Philip Whitcomb is a private client partner at Moore Barlow LLP. He acts for a large number of farmers and landowners and specialises in advising on succession planning and the structuring of farm businesses. His approach is to give practical and workable solutions to clients taking into account their circumstances and particular needs and wishes. Philip is a Fellow of the Agricultural Law Association and a member of the Country Land and Business Association. He regularly lectures nationally to professionals on capital taxation, Wills, trusts and farming business structures. As well as being on the editorial board for Farm Tax Briefing and a contributor to Stanley's Taxation of Farmers and Landowners.

He enjoys gardening and antique collecting and lives in Dorset with his wife, Alison.

A Practical Guide to the Law of Farming Partnerships

A Practical Guide to the Law of Farming Partnerships

Philip Whitcomb
Partner, Moore Barlow LLP
BA (Hons), FALA

Law Brief Publishing

© Philip Whitcomb

All rights reserved. No part of this publication may be reproduced, stored in a retrieval system, or transmitted, in any form or by any means, electronic, mechanical, photocopying, recording or otherwise, without the prior permission of the publisher.

Excerpts from judgments and statutes are Crown copyright. Any Crown Copyright material is reproduced with the permission of the Controller of OPSI and the Queen's Printer for Scotland. Some quotations may be licensed under the terms of the Open Government Licence (http://www.nationalarchives.gov.uk/doc/open-government-licence/version/3).

Cover image © iStockphoto.com/JamesBrey

The information in this book was believed to be correct at the time of writing. All content is for information purposes only and is not intended as legal advice. No liability is accepted by either the publisher or author for any errors or omissions (whether negligent or not) that it may contain. Professional advice should always be obtained before applying any information to particular circumstances.

Published 2020 by Law Brief Publishing, an imprint of Law Brief Publishing Ltd
30 The Parks
Minehead
Somerset
TA24 8BT

www.lawbriefpublishing.com

Paperback: 978-1-912687-32-9

For my wife, Alison

PREFACE

Many professionals will be familiar with partnerships and how they work but few will truly understand the nuances and complexities of a farming partnership. In the past this may not have mattered but with high values of land and an increasingly elderly farming population, the risk levels for advising in this area of the law have increased significantly.

Recognising the key problems that many farming families face, the need for commerciality and succession planning, this book explores the practical legal issues through a number of topics centred around the different aspects of a farming partnership. All farming partnerships are tailor-made to meet the specific circumstances of the client. The purpose of this book is to give an overview, with practical examples, of the main issues that you may come across. Whilst it does not have the scope to consider all the case law in relation to partnerships in detail, it does provide the main points, guidelines and strategies to help and support all those involved in advising on farming partnerships.

The law quoted in this edition is accurate as at 30 July 2020, including coverage of all statutes, statutory instruments, court cases, tribunal decisions, online announcements/guidance, statements of practice, concessions, HMRC Manuals, HMRC Briefs and other publications.

I welcome all comments and suggestions of improvements to this work.

Philip Whitcomb
July 2020

CONTENTS

Chapter One	Partnerships in the Farming Context	1
	1.1. Introduction	1
	1.2. The Holistic Approach	4
	1.3. General Characteristics	5
	1.4. The issue of legal personality	6
	1.5. Choice of Partnership	7
	1.5.1. General Partnerships	7
	1.5.2. Limited Partnerships	8
	1.5.3. Limited Liability Partnerships	9
	1.6. The role of the professional	10
	1.7. Negligence claims and risk	11
Chapter Two	Formation of a Farming Partnership and the Need for an Updated Agreement	13
	2.1. The question of whether a partnership agreement exists	13
	2.2. What is a Partnership	15
	2.3. A business	15
	2.4. Being carried on by two or more persons in common	16
	2.5. With a view of profit	17
	2.6. Presumptions in determining a partnership	18
	2.7. No requirement for a written partnership agreement	19
	2.8. Limited Partnership formation	20
	2.9. Limited Liability Partnership formation	20
Chapter Three	Property and the Use of the Land Capital Account	21
	3.1. Land as partnership property	21
	3.2. The historic problem of land in partnerships	22
	3.3. Land used by the partnership but held outside it	24
	3.4. Licence	25
	3.5. Licence arrangements for Limited Partners	26
	3.6. Lease arrangement	26

	3.7.	Agricultural Holdings Act Tenancy	27
	3.8.	Assignment of an Agricultural Holdings Act Tenancy to a partnership	29
	3.9.	Landowner entering into partnership with non-landowning partner – use of a licence	30
	3.10.	Farm Business Tenancy	31
	3.11.	Terms of the tenancy arrangement	31
	3.12.	Continuance of the Lease on dissolution of the Partnership	32
	3.13.	Land owned by the partnership	33
	3.14.	Absence of agreement on what is partnership property	35
	3.15.	Purchase of new land during the duration of the partnership	36
	3.16.	Improvements to Property	38
	3.17.	Execution of Deeds	39
	3.18.	Limited Liability Partnerships	39
Chapter Four	**General Capital and Finance**		**41**
	4.1.	What is capital?	41
	4.2.	Interest on capital contributions	42
	4.3.	What is included in the general capital of a farming partnership	43
	4.4.	The assumption of equality	44
	4.5.	Accounting treatment of undrawn profits	46
	4.6.	Losses	46
	4.7.	Loans to the Partnership	47
	4.8.	Partnership Books and Accounts	47
	4.9.	Limited Partnerships	48
	4.10.	Limited Liability Partnerships	48
	4.11.	Rectification of farm partnership accounts	49
Chapter Five	**Division of Profits and Losses**		**51**
	5.1.	The presumption of equality for capital	52
	5.2.	Right to a share of income profits	52
	5.3.	Division of income profits	53
	5.4.	Entitlement to withdraw	55
	5.5.	Losses of an income nature	56
	5.6.	Accounts and allocation of profits	56

Chapter Six	Management and Decision Making		57
	6.1.	Right to management	57
	6.2.	Management by "farming" partners	58
	6.3.	Decision making process by a majority of partners	59
	6.4.	Equal number of votes and deadlock	60
	6.5.	Rights of minority and acting in good faith	60
	6.6.	Unanimous decisions	61
	6.7.	Delegation of management function	62
	6.8.	Limited Partnerships	62
	6.9.	Limited Liability Partnerships	63
Chapter Seven	Death of a Farmer		65
	7.1.	Statutory presumption on death of a Partner	65
	7.2.	Position of a sole surviving partner	66
	7.3.	Personal Representatives becoming partners in the Business	67
	7.4.	Technical dissolution	69
	7.5.	General dissolution	69
	7.6.	The nature of the deceased's partner's interest	70
	7.7.	Sale of the deceased's share to the surviving partners	71
	7.8.	Use of life assurance	74
	7.9.	Post dissolution profits and section 42 of the Partnership Act, 1890	75
	7.10.	Valuation of the outgoing deceased Partner's share	78
	7.11.	Valuation of Agricultural Holdings Act Tenancies	80
	7.12.	Debts of the Partnership	83
	7.13.	Partner's Wills	83
	7.14.	Potential increase in the costs of Probate fees	86
	7.15.	Key decisions of the personal representatives	86
Chapter Eight	Succession Planning of the Family Farm and the Use of Partnerships		89
	8.1.	Parties to the agreement and recitals	89
	8.2.	Commencement and duration of the partnership	90
	8.3.	Nature of the business	90

	8.4.	Retirement	91
	8.5.	Banking	91
	8.6.	Books and Accounts	92
	8.7.	Expulsion	92
	8.8.	Assignment of a Partnership Share	93
	8.9.	Asset protection clauses	94

Chapter Nine	Capacity Issues and the Elderly Farmer		97
	9.1.	Family member joining into a partnership with fluctuating capacity	98
	9.2.	Existing partner in a farming partnership loses capacity	100
	9.3.	Powers of Attorney	101
	9.4.	Delegation authority	104
	9.5.	Position if a person has lost capacity – entering into a partnership	104
	9.6.	The importance of the protection of APR & BPR if a partner loses capacity	106
	9.7.	Ability to dissolve a partnership	107
	9.8.	Authority to transfer partnership capital	107
	9.9.	Conflicts of interest	109

Chapter Ten	Dissolution of the Business		111
	10.1.	Reasons for dissolution	111
	10.2.	Serving notice	112
	10.3.	Express clauses and mutual agreement	114
	10.4.	Court Order	114
	10.5.	Winding up of the partnership business	116
	10.6.	Application of assets on a winding up	117
	10.7.	Buy out or Syers v Syers orders	118
	10.8.	Arbitration and Mediation	119
	10.9.	Proprietary Estoppel Claims	120

Chapter Eleven	Stamp Duty Land Tax		123
	11.1.	Transfer of a chargeable interest to a partnership	124
	11.2.	Transfer of a partnership interest to another partner	125
	11.3.	Transfer of land from a partnership	126
	11.4.	The three year anti avoidance rule	126

Chapter Twelve	IHT & CGT		129
	12.1.	Agricultural Property Relief – the basics	129
	12.2.	More than one farmhouse	133
	12.3.	Haymaking and Partnerships	133
	12.4.	Atkinson and the Ailing Farmer	134
	12.5.	Partnership Property, Capital Gains Tax and the Farmhouse	136
	12.6.	Business Property Relief	137
	12.7.	Rates of Business Property Relief which apply to partnerships	138
	12.8.	The mixed farming estate	139
	12.9.	Capital Gains Tax and Partnerships	140
	12.10.	Business Asset Disposal Relief	141
	12.11.	Holdover Relief	142
	12.12.	Rollover Relief	142
	12.13.	Farmhouses and Rollover Relief	143
	12.14.	Partitions of Joint Interests in Land	143
	12.15.	Gifts with reservation of benefit	145
Chapter Thirteen	The Use of Limited Partnerships and Limited Liability Partnerships		147
	13.1.	Limited Partnerships	147
	13.2.	Use of Limited Partnerships in a farming context	148
	13.3.	Forfeiture of limited liability	149
	13.4.	Limited Liability Partnerships	150
	13.5.	Use of Limited Liability Partnerships in a farming context	151
Chapter Fourteen	Income Tax		153
	14.1.	Farming income as a trade	153
	14.2.	The taxation of profits of a farming partnership	154
	14.3.	Expenditure of a capital or income nature	154
	14.4.	Profit averaging	156
	14.5.	Farm losses and sideways loss relief	158
	14.6.	Reporting issues when there is a partnership dispute	159

CHAPTER ONE
PARTNERSHIPS IN THE
FARMING CONTEXT

1.1 Introduction

It is a fact, universally acknowledged amongst professional advisors, that a farming business which is run as a partnership, is in want of a decent partnership agreement. That is an agreement in writing, which reflects not only the nuances of conducting an agricultural business on the land but also the circumstances, dynamics and aspirations of the current partners.

This is not always a message which is readily received by farmers, who are traditionally comfortable with conducting their businesses on a handshake. It has been estimated that 10% of all businesses are carried on by traditional partnerships, but in the farming sector that percentage is significantly higher. The concerning point is that because of the traditional way farms have conducted their businesses, those with a written partnership agreement or an up to date partnership agreement are worryingly low. Then there is the added dimension that, in most cases, the co-partners are members of the family. If you cannot trust your family who can you trust? What could possibly go wrong, after all blood is thicker than water? The answer, of course, is that it is just these types of arrangements which can go spectacularly wrong. In the last few years there have been a number of legal cases where there was either no partnership agreement or the agreement did not cover appropriately the circumstance that had arisen.

In the Court of Appeal decision of *Ham v Ham (2013) EWCA Civ 1301* Lord Justice Briggs commented on the interpretation of particular clauses within a written farming partnership agreement that *"it is unhappily common for this type of issue not to be clearly dealt with in partnership agreements. It is an obvious problem in relation to farming partnerships, where the land forms an asset of the firm. It is hoped that, in future, those preparing such agreements will take note of the anxiety, expense and delay which such unnecessary uncertainty can cause"*. This case concerned a 178-hectare dairy farm in Frome, Somerset in which the partners consisted of Ron and Jean Ham (husband and wife), and their son, John. The business began in 1966 and John joined the partnership in 1997. The hope and intention of the parents was for John to one day inherit the farm and carry on the business. At first everyone worked well together but by 2009 it was clear that there were material differences on the strategy of the future of the farm. John wanted to drive the farm in one direction, his parents disagreed and refused to relinquish control. As a result, John resigned from the partnership citing irreconcilable differences with his parents. Under the terms of the partnership agreement, the remaining partners had an option to purchase the outgoing partner's share. The question and difficulty in this particular case was the value to be assigned to that partner's share. The written partnership agreement was poorly worded using the unhelpful phrase of "net value" to be agreed between the partners and, in default of agreement, by the accountants acting as experts. Ron and Jean Ham claimed that the value should be assessed on the book value of the assets as recorded in the accounts - a rather low amount as it did not take into account the rise in property values of the preceding ten years. John argued that it was the open market value of the assets at the time of his resignation. The Court of Appeal agreed with John's interpretation on the facts of the case that the open market value should be used and not the historic costs as his parents understood.

How many poorly drafted farming partnerships are out there with such phrasing? How often does the partnership agreement not help the circumstances facing the family, or even more likely, there is no partnership agreement at all? With so much at stake why are there not more good quality agreements out there? Is it an unwillingness of the client to pay the costs or is it an unwillingness to face up to making potentially difficult decisions?

Even if the partnership agreement does contain well drafted provisions, that does not necessarily mean litigation between family members will be avoided, but it can certainly help to defend such a claim. This has been shown in the recent case of *Horsford v Horsford (2020) EWHC 584 (Ch)* which involved a claim by mother for payment for her share of the farming partnership upon her retirement. Mother and son had farmed in partnership since the 1980s. Initially with the son's father but since 2012 the partners were just mother and son. They had a written partnership agreement which had taken several months of discussions and negotiations to put in place. The agreement dealt with the issues of retirement of a partner, options for the remaining partners to purchase the outgoing partner's share and the methodology of how to calculate the value of that share. In 2016, the mother served notice to retire and the son served notice to purchase her share in accordance with the partnership agreement. As payment for the mother's share (valued at £2.52 million) wasn't forthcoming the mother brought proceedings to enforce payment. The son counter-claimed disputing some elements of the land valuation, the payment of expert fees and on the grounds of equity arising by proprietary estoppel.

Whilst various assurances had taken place over the years by the mother on the inheritance of the farm by the son, it was found that he had not really suffered a detriment but actually had benefitted from his parents' generosity. Even if he had acquired any such equity, he had the right to acquire his mother's share in the partnership pursuant to clause 19 of the partnership agreement. The agreement also provided that its terms were "*deemed to have governed the affairs and operation of the partnership*" and that it constituted "*the whole of the agreement between the partners as to the business*". The partnership agreement was therefore intended to record all of the parties' rights and obligations and so any rights inconsistent with the rights as recorded were extinguished. This is particularly true in a case such as this, where the partnership agreement was prepared over several months and both parties were clear on the rights and responsibilities under it. As a consequence the case was found in favour of the mother.

1.2 The Holistic Approach

In the past preparation of a farming partnership was traditionally dealt with by the corporate commercial team within a legal practice. Often this is still the case but there is a recent trend for private client practitioners also to be intrinsically involved. The reason for this is simple. The primary motivations for farming businesses putting in place an up to date partnership agreement include a drive to undertake succession planning and/or capital taxation mitigation strategies. It is not just the lawyers who should, or need to be, involved in advising the farmer client on the creation and running of the farming partnership business; the accountant and land agent also have skills and the expertise to add value to the proceedings. All good advice is achieved when an holistic approach is adopted; drawing in the specialisms of the accountant, lawyer and land agent. No one professional could or indeed should be working in silo. Still, if you strip the task at hand back to basics, this is a legal document and as such it will be the lawyer who will be required to take the lead role calling on the expertise of the other professionals.

There is also the temptation to put to one side those elements which need addressing but due to circumstances, indecision or lack of communication between partners end up in the "too difficult to think about" category. Those inexperienced in dealing with this or in an effort just to get the matter over the line, may therefore not address these points adequately in the partnership agreement. Such points as:

- How will the sweat equity of the younger generation be rewarded?

- What happens on the death of a partner?

- How will the value of an outgoing partner be valued?

- How will non-farming partners be recompensed?

- What happens if a partner losses mental capacity?

- What would happen in the event of a dispute between partners?

The temptation by both the client and the professional to place some or all of these questions in the "too difficult to think about" category should be resisted. Whilst it may seem expedient to do so in the short term, and often with the intention to revisit, human nature such as it is, the chances are you may never get around to doing it until it is too late. As we shall see, it is questions around these issues which has become the subject of litigation between partners and that cannot be in the interests of any client.

1.3 General Characteristics

Section 1(1) of the Partnership Act, 1890 is remarkable in the simplicity of a definition of a partnership as a *"relation which subsists between persons carrying on a business with a view to profit"*. The definition contains three key ingredients for a partnership but the key word is "relation". It is all about relationships. A relationship between the partners themselves. A contract between individuals, similar to a marriage. All marriages have ups and downs and it is only when the marriage goes wrong does anyone look at any pre-nuptial or post-nuptial agreement. The same applies with a partnership agreement and that is why the partnership agreement is vital. Nobody looks at the legal documentation when things are going well, but it will be scrutinised carefully when the relationship breaks down. As well as the governance of the internal relationships between partners, there is also a relationship and interaction with the outside world and the legislation and the partnership agreement has to govern those relationships as well as the internal ones.

All partnerships, whether farming or not, have three main characteristics and when preparing a new partnership agreement or advising on partners' rights and obligations, it is always worth having these fundamental characteristics in mind. The first characteristic is that a partnership is a contract upon which the law implies certain terms and obligations towards third parties. Some of these terms may be varied by express agreement by the partners (for those terms which govern the relationship between those co-partners) and by express agreement by the third party (for those terms which govern the relation between that third party). The key point here is that it is an express variation. The second characteristic is that there is an obligation of good faith between partners. This may seem quite a basic point in that if partners do not trust each other not to work against the interests of the partnership, then is there really a partnership at all? As has already been stated, a partnership is a relationship between individuals and for it to succeed it must be based on mutual confidence and trust between the partners. You do not have to like your fellow partners. Partnerships can work just as effectively without the partners liking each other but even in these cases each partner must be just and faithful in his or her dealings with the partnership business. This brings us neatly to the third characteristic. A partnership is a commercial undertaking; it is a business and the motivation behind entering into a partnership is to make a profit, otherwise what is the point. Granted, you may not always do so and in farming that is often the case, but the reason for going into a partnership and staying in a partnership is with the aspiration that a profit from the farming business will be forthcoming.

1.4 The issue of legal personality

Unlike Scottish partnerships, partnerships governed by the law of England and Wales do not have a legal personality. They only have relationships between partners and third parties. The agreement and statute governs those relationships. This presents a certain amount of confusion because they look like a corporate entity. The trading name is often something like J Bloggs & Son; they can sue and be sued in the name of the partnership; and tax assessments are raised in the name of the firm. Section 4(1) of the Partnership Act, 1890 even refers to a partnership by the common shorthand of a "firm". Yet despite this, the fundamentals of partnerships are based on contract law and the relationship between one partner and his or her fellow partners as well as the partnership's relationship with the outside world.

1.5 Choice of Partnership

There are three types of partnerships which tend to be found in an agricultural context.

1.5.1 General Partnerships

By far the most common type of farming partnership is the general partnership, governed by the Partnership Act, 1890. About 90% of farm partnerships you will come across fall into this category. The fact that the principle governing statute is 130 years old can sometimes present problems if the partnership agreement has not dealt with the issue.

The Act itself, was and is, largely declaratory of the law containing a number of default rules as well as a number of mandatory ones. It is not a codifying or a consolidating Act in that section 46 of the Partnership Act, 1890 preserves all equitable and common law rules applicable to partnerships *"except so far as they are inconsistent with the express provisions of this Act"*. It is a short Act with only fifty sections. The default provisions (governing the mutual rights and duties between the partners) can be excluded or amended by the partnership agreement; the mandatory ones (which centre around third party rights) cannot. This demonstrates the contractual relationship of a partnership. The Act covers three main areas; the relations between those third-party rights; the relations between the partners themselves and thirdly the dissolution and winding up of the partnership.

As well as the partners being able to vary their mutual rights and duties as laid down in the Partnership Act, 1890 by express consent, they can also be varied through implied consent by their actions. In the absence of a partnership agreement this course of dealing could be evidenced by the annual accounts and that is why a good set of accounts, which accords with the terms of the partnership agreement, and what is happening on the ground is vital. In the case of *Ham v Bell (2016) EWHC 1791 (Ch)* (a case we will look at in greater detail in this book) the role the accounts and the accountant played helped to illuminate the implied terms of the partnership.

1.5.2 Limited Partnerships

Whilst there are approximately 23,000 Limited Partnerships in the UK, until very recently these partnerships were rarely seen in the farming partnership context. They have gained popularity as the entity used to deal with instances where professionals (most commonly as trustees) also need to be partners in the farming business. Suppose a farmer wishes to bring his children into the farming business after his death but is concerned that if he dies in the next few years they would be too young and inexperienced to take on, the full mantle of responsibility. In the light of this he decides in his Will to have a discretionary trust and to appoint his accountant and his lawyer (as the family's trusted advisors) as trustees. His primary wish in the letter of wishes, which accompanies his Will, is for the farming business to continue with his children involved but also for the trustees to have a guiding hand. One way to perhaps achieve this is through a Limited Partnership, where the trustees' liability would be limited to the value of the partnership assets. It is, of course, important that the trustees have the relevant powers under the trust deed or Will.

The other main use of Limited Partners in a farming context is to involve non-farming members in the farming business, particularly if they have an interest in the underlying land. Take the example of Pippa, Tom and Daniel. Following the death of their father, Harry, the family farm was left in equal shares to his three children. The siblings get on well together but it is only Daniel who is actively interested in farming. Are they storing up trouble for the future if there is no agreement to regulate their arrangements? Both Pippa and Tom have careers away from the farm but they still wish to feel involved in the farm and to protect their inheritance tax position on their respective deaths. A Limited Partnership allows Pippa and Tom to be limited partners in the partnership and so feel involved as stakeholders but they are not involved with the day to day management of the farm. This is left to Daniel as the unlimited partner. This arrangement meets Daniel's wishes to be left alone to farm and also Pippa's and Tom's wishes to maximise the Agricultural Property Relief and Business Property Relief position in the event of their deaths. Effectively, Pippa and Tom as stakeholders would be sleeping partners and allow Daniel to manage and run the farm.

The Limited Partnership works in very much the same ways as a traditional partnership. The difference is that it is possible for one or more partners to join into the partnership but their liability is only limited to the capital they have actually introduced. There has to be one or more general partners (in the above example it was Daniel) who has unlimited liability and it is the unlimited partners who have the management of the partnership.

The other difference with a Limited Partnership is that it has to be registered at Companies House. Details include the name, nature of business, place of business, name of each partner, commencement date, statement that this is a limited partnership and particulars of each limited partner, but importantly not the annual accounts. It therefore has more confidentiality than a Limited Liability Partnership and appeals to many farmers who do not wish their profits or losses to be made public knowledge.

The Limited Partnership is still governed by the Partnerships Act, 1890 but as modified by the Limited Partnerships Act, 1907 and supplemented by the Limited Partnerships (Forms) Rules, 2009.

1.5.3 Limited Liability Partnerships

Probably the most familiar type of partnerships for professionals (because most professional service partnerships are them) are Limited Liability Partnerships. There are 59,000 registered Limited Liability Partnerships in the UK but ironically there are far less common for our agricultural clients. Technically they are not even a partnership in the truest sense but a body corporate with members instead of partners. A sort of hybrid between a company and a partnership. Section 1(5) of the Limited Liability Partnership Act, 2000 expressly excludes most partnership law from applying and so Limited Liability Partnerships have more in common with Company Law then Partnership Law. The Partnership Act, 1890 does not apply to Limited Liability Partnerships. In other words, the approach is devised from applied company law with distinct partnership elements. Unlike a company, however, there are no directors, shareholders or share capital. In general terms a member of the Limited Liability Partnership is liable only to the extent of the capital introduced and undrawn profits. Where they arise in an agricultural context is where the business, in whole or in part, has an element of high risk and the client wishes to limit the risk to the assets within the partnership. A good example of this in a landed estate context would be the running of an aerodrome, which potentially has a high risk of liability if things go wrong.

Unlike General Partnerships and Limited Partnerships, the Limited Liability Partnership is governed by the Limited Liability Partnership Act 2000 which sets out the framework of an LLP. The detailed governing regulations are contained in the Limited Liability Partnerships Regulations, 2001 (SI 2001/1090) as amended by the Limited Liability Partnerships (Application of Companies Act, 2006) Regulations, 2009.

Where Limited Liability Partnerships can add value and flexibility in terms of funding is that Limited Liability Partnerships can offer the security of a floating charge which a General or Limited Partnership cannot. Thereby offering better security for lenders.

1.6   The role of the professional

Time spent considering and preparing a partnership agreement is time worth spending. There is a tendency for clients to think that these agreements are straightforward and, since it is family, any issues (if they ever arose) would be dealt with by discussions around the kitchen table. Yet often they are not straightforward and part of the role of the professional is to challenge this view and get the family to consider scenarios that they may not have thought of, or have considered, would arise. It is essential for existing partners and new partners coming into the farming business to agree how decisions are to be made and what will happen if one of them leaves or dies. Most importantly the vision for the future of the farming business needs to be discussed so that the partners are clear on everyone's intentions. This very point was demonstrated in the *Ham v Ham* and *Horsford v Horsford* cases where it did not happen. Like most disputes it is the lack of communication and misunderstandings which are at the root cause. A classic example of this, and one seen in many cases where the relationship has broken down, is where the senior partners (the ones who have been farming the land for many years) have perhaps a more traditional farming policy whilst the more junior partners may wish to take the business in a new innovative direction. The root cause of *Ham v Ham* is just this type of disagreement. It is only with a challenging and searching approach that these potential future flash points become apparent.

Striking the right balance between the interests and views of the more elderly partners and the interests of the junior partners requires open communication and in some cases diplomacy. The issue of conflicts of interest and whether one faction should be separately represented should be at the forefront of the professional's mind. This is particularly relevant where you have farming and non-farming members of the family perhaps with the non-farming members getting those assets outside of the farming business. For good sound reasons the profits from the farming business could be reinvested into the business but if that is to the detriment of investing that money in non-farming investments which would benefit the non-farming members of the family in the future and it was done on the back of the advice from the professional, is there not a potential risk of a claim by the non-farming members of the family in the future who have lost out as a result?

The creation of a new partnership agreement needs to be an informed process where each person is fully aware of the rights and obligations that they are entering into. No matter how well the partnership agreement has been drafted if the parties do not understand what they are entering into then it has the potential to fail.

1.7 Negligence claims and risk

Land values over the last twenty years have risen significantly. With such high values and the increasing specialism of farming professional advice, there are risks for those generalists straying into advising farmers on an ad hoc basis. The chances of getting it wrong significantly increase. Whatever the motivation for creating a partnership or adapting one already in existence, it is important to record on the file the intentions from the client, clear notes of any meetings and any advice on risk. Particularly important when advising on family partnerships is to step back and assess who your client actually is. Is it all of the partners or just some of them, say, the senior generation? Is there a need for the new partners to seek their own independent legal advice?

There is no harm in seeking specialist advice on aspects of your work for a client. In fact, in the case of *Mehjoo v Harben Barker (a firm) (2014) EWCA Civ 358* it was emphasised that there exists a duty of care to refer clients to specialists where the need arises. Farming Partnerships are one area where there can be clear examples of the need to obtain specialist advice if appropriate. Examples could include assessing whether the land is owned by individual partners or as partnership property or the treatment of the partnership assets on the death of a partner. Otherwise there is a risk of straying into unfamiliar territory and providing inaccurate advice.

Whilst the family may have the right intentions in the event of a disagreement, it is not until the partnership agreement is actually signed and completed that those terms which you laboured over are able to bind the partners. This may seem a crazy point to raise but it can happen that the partnership agreement is created but the farming family never get around to signing it and the professionals do not chase it up. Such a fact arose in the proprietary estoppel case of *Davies v Davies (2014) EXCA Civ 568* where the partnership agreement remained unsigned even though the parties had, by conduct, followed its terms. It is beholden on all professionals to ensure these documents are in place and have been signed. Accountants especially, are uniquely placed to assist as they have the advantage of having regular meetings with the clients to sign accounts and tax returns. This is a great opportunity whilst everyone is together and focussed to raise the need to complete any outstanding documentation which affords good legal protection for the entire family.

CHAPTER TWO
FORMATION OF A FARMING PARTNERSHIP AND THE NEED FOR AN UPDATED AGREEMENT

2.1 The question of whether a partnership exists

Whether or not a partnership exists is a question of fact; the essence being a continuing commercial relationship between two or more parties. Often the relationship is governed by a contractual arrangement (the partnership agreement) but this is not necessarily the case and there are many farming businesses which are run without any written partnership agreement. The key is to look at the substance of the arrangements and not the stated intentions of the parties.

This is probably best illustrated with an example. An equine business is set up by a son on land owned by the parents originally on a landlord/tenant basis. Time passes and the son needs finance to develop the business and this can only be done with the land being held as security. So the parents agree to go into partnership with the son instead and the mortgage documentation is signed on that basis. No partnership agreement is signed though one is prepared and the bank account remains in the sole name of the son. Six months later the accountant queried whether a partnership was in existence. The answer is that there is a partnership because on the facts the substance of the arrangements (entering into a mortgage arrangement) the parties had embarked on a business activity i.e. to develop the equine business. Assets had been acquired, liabilities incurred and expenditure laid out in the course of the joint venture and with the consent of both the parents and the son.

In the above example, the trading business had already begun as a sole trade and had metamorphosed into a partnership arrangement. However it is important to distinguish between people working together with a concept of a business but no means to create a profit, with those actually carrying on a business with a view to profit. Two people may have the desire to run an Alpaca farm and to sell the meat and wool but if they have not actually purchased the alpacas and merely undertaken preparatory investigatory work then this is not a business. In the case of *Illot v Williams & Others (2013) EWCA Civ 645* there was a concept of a business but no means to make a profit. It is not enough to simply identify the business on which the parties had agreed to embark (in this case an asset management business) but whether they had actually done enough to have commenced the business. In this case there was no evidence that the parties had made any financial commitment and no assurance of funding or regulatory approval. Importantly there was no evidence that any party had sought to bind the other parties.

If there is a partnership agreement then it will usually state within it a commencement date as to when the partnership business began. This is not necessarily the date of the agreement itself but can be an earlier date as agreed between the parties. If there is no partnership agreement, and even when there is, it may be important to establish the date upon which the business started. This can be useful for tax purposes, for example to meet the qualifying period to obtain Entrepreneurs' Relief (now Business Asset Disposal Relief) for capital gains tax purposes or to bind the partners to their obligations. Again, it is a question of fact and for these purposes there is a distinction between running a business in common once the preliminary work had been done and taking preparatory steps before actually trading - a twilight period during which the legal relationships are being determined. This point was demonstrated in the case of *Khan v Miah (2001) 1 ALL ER 20* where the House of Lords held that the parties had done enough to have commenced the joint enterprise in which they had agreed to engage. The partners had acquired the property, in this case a restaurant, and had undertaken preparatory work including paying for building contractors to convert the premises, a loan had been taken out and furniture and equipment had been purchased. Even though the restaurant never opened before the relationship between the parties broke down, enough had been done for a partnership to have been formed. Where this may also become relevant in a farming context is when a sole trade farmer invites a child (or children) to come into the business with him and this could quickly develop into a partnership relationship, even if the intentions of the parties were not so to do at the beginning. The intentions of the parties are not material to whether a partnership is in existence. As stated, it is necessary to look at the substance of the relationship. So perhaps in this case the younger generation have diversified part of the farming business into a new arrangement, say jointly taking out finance with the parent to fund the new enterprise. Any profits, or any intended profits, to be ploughed into the one business. It is easy to see a slippery slope for the farming business to change from being held as a sole trade to a partnership arrangement.

2.2 What is a partnership?

Section 1(1) of the Partnership Act, 1890 defines a partnership as one *"which subsists between persons carrying on a business in common with a view of profit"*. A business will only acquire the legal status of a partnership if the three conditions are met and is automatic, even if the parties had not intended for there to be one. The three conditions contained in section 1(1) of the Partnership Act, 1890 are:

1. There must be a business;

2. Which is being carried on by two or more persons in common; and

3. With a view of profit.

2.3 A business

This may seem straightforward and obvious and section 45 of the Partnership Act, 1890 defines a business as including *"every trade, occupation or profession"* but not all activity undertaken on land constitutes a business. A common scenario in the rural world would be equine sporting activities being undertaken on the property. The First-Tier case of *Sir Keith Mills, Team Origin LLP v HMRC (2017) TC05844* considered whether sporting businesses can be deemed as trading. This case related to a Limited Liability Partnership which was set up as an entity for assembling a sailing team to win the America's Cup international sailing competition but the same issues and questions would equally apply to an equine sporting enterprise. The First Tier Tribunal held that not only the racing element but also the activity of obtaining sponsorships was trading. In the case of *Eugene Blaney v Revenue & Customs (2014) UKFTT 1001 (TC)* the badges of trade approach was used in determining whether or not horse breeding activities amounted to a trade. In this case it was held that the operation was too small to constitute a trade and that the prime motivation was the owner's lover of horses and horse racing. However, if a farm is being purchased for the purposes of starting a business this may be sufficient. In the case of *Khan v Miah,* Lord Millett indicates that the purchase or lease of the business premises was sufficient to have created a partnership.

2.4   Being carried on by two or more persons in common

For there to be a partnership there needs to be one or more persons involved. If one person is left it cannot, by definition, be a partnership but a sole trade. Under the Interpretation Act, 1978 a "Person" includes individuals, companies and limited liability partnerships. The involvement is participation in the business as opposed to a mere connection with a business. In *Strathearn Gordon Associates Ltd v Commissioner of Customs & Excise (1985) VATTR 79* the company acted as management consultants on seven separate development sites. Whilst part of the agreement was that as well as their fees being paid, they would share some of the profits, the parties had made no agreement to carry on a business together. The essence of the agreement was a provision of services and was not actual participation in the development business. There were two separate businesses bearing their own risks but with a mutual interest. The same analogy can be used to distinguish a share farming arrangement from a farming partnership. The former is the coming together of two parties in a mutually beneficial agreement to farm an area of land whilst remaining as two separate businesses. There are no guaranteed payments, regardless of business performance but an assessment of the value of the assets used and expertise each

2. FORMATION OF PARTNERSHIP & NEED FOR AN UPDATED AGREEMENT • 17

person is bringing to the table. A farming partnership, by contrast, is the coming together of two persons to form a single business entity to farm an area of land. There is one business in which profits or losses are divided in accordance with what the parties have agreed. When the share farming arrangement ends, each party just walks away; in a farming partnership the business is dissolved and the net assets are divided between the parties as per the agreement.

The parties in a share farming arrangement do not participate in the management of each other's businesses. As shall be seen later, in accordance with section 24(5) of the Partnership Act, 1890, each partner may take part in the management of the business. In other words, they have the right to be involved in the management of the firm even if they chose by agreement not to. This is a fundamental aspect of the phrase "in common"; a right to exercise the management role. A right that sets a partnership apart from a share farming agreement. In *Saywell v Pope (1979) 53 TC 40* the wives of the existing partners were held not to be partners prior to 1975 in the firm dealing in and repairing agricultural machinery because they had taken a passive role, and had never been integrated into the partnership including being involved in the management of the firm. That does not mean that a partner has to be involved in management in order to be a partner, just the right and ability to do so if the respective partner so choses. The exception to the participation requirement in the management relates to a limited partner in a Limited Partnership. Such a person is forbidden to take part in the management of the firm if they wish to retain their limited liability status.

2.5   With a view of profit

The final element is an intention to make a profit from the business undertaken. That does not necessarily mean that you have to make a profit year on year. There will be a large percentage of farming partnerships which would fail on that criteria. The key point is an intention to do so. This lies at the very heart of a partnership relationship. The prime motivation of entering into the relationship is to make a financial return on the investment. It can hardly be a partnership if this is not contemplated.

2.6 Presumptions in determining a partnership

Section 1 of the Partnership Act, 1890 provides the essential criteria required to have a partnership but it is section 2 which gives some flesh to the bones by giving a number of presumptions in determining whether there is a partnership. It is intended to be of practical assistance when dealing with specific situations. Section 2(1) of the Partnership Act, 1890 confirms that mere joint ownership of property does not in itself create a partnership. Many farms will be legally owned by more than one person but there needs to be more for the legal owners to have a farming partnership. If the legal owners let the land then the activity of letting property could mean they can form a partnership to run a rental business. More common in farming situations would be for the legal owners letting the property to a farming partnership business on a formal Farm Business Tenancy or an Agricultural Holdings Act Tenancy. The farming business are the ones occupying the land and running the activity of farming from it.

The sharing of gross profits is not sufficient to prove the existence of a partnership, but section 2(2) of the Partnership Act, 1890 does provide that the sharing of net profits would be good evidence of the existence of a partnership. In the case of *Cox v Coulson (1916) 2 KB 177* two parties in a joint theatrical venture who shared gross box office receipts and paid separately the various expenses they had each incurred was held not to be sufficient evidence of a partnership. As we have already seen there is a close analogy here with a Share Farming Arrangement which is also not a Partnership.

The main force, however, in section 2 is section 2(3) which considers the connection between receiving a financial return from a business and the creation of a partnership. There are a variety of relationships which can exist in which monies can be paid from the returns from a business without a partnership being formed. These include a debtor/creditor relationship, an employer and employee relationship and a lender and borrower relationship.

2.7 No requirement for a written partnership agreement

There is no legal requirement to have a written partnership agreement or indeed to put anything in writing. Despite the requirements of section 2 of the Law of Property (Miscellaneous Provisions) Act, 1989 even if the partnership involved interests in land there is no requirement for a written partnership agreement. Many farming partnerships exist quite happily without anything in writing. The problem comes when certainty over terms is needed or the partners do not wish it or it is disadvantageous for the default provisions as set out in the Partnership Act, 1890, to apply.

Regardless of whether there is a written agreement or not, the Courts are more concerned with the substance of the relationship rather than any written statement. Just because there is a statement stating that this is a partnership, it does not make it so, if on closer examination it is not really a partnership relationship at all. When there is a written agreement, it will usually take the form of a deed setting out the main partnership provisions and terms upon which the relationship is to be conducted. It can vary the rights and duties of the partners. Section 19 of the Partnership Act, 1890 states that "*the mutual rights and duties of the partners, whether ascertained by agreement or defined by this Act, may be varied by the consent of all the partners, and such consent may be either express or inferred from a course of dealing*". In the case of *Pilling v Pilling (1865) 46 ER 599* the written agreement was effectively ignored for eleven years on the allocation of profits and it was held this was sufficient to vary the agreement through a course of dealing. If, however, the partnership agreement states that any amendments have to be in writing then that will effectively displace the provisions of section 19 of the Partnership Act, 1890 in that the agreement cannot then be altered by "*a course of dealing*".

2.8 Limited Partnership formation

Section 1 of the Partnership Act, 1890 applies to Limited Partnerships as well. The two key differences, as detailed elsewhere in this book, is that there must be at least one general partner and the partnership must be registered at Companies House. Section 8 of the Limited Partnerships Act, 1907 requires all the partners to sign the statement of registration but no written partnership agreement is required. It is quite possible to have a limited partnership without any form of agreement but you must have registered the entity at Companies House.

2.9 Limited Liability Partnership formation

In order for a Limited Liability Partnership to be created, it must be incorporated by registration at Companies House. Registration includes not only the submission of an incorporation document but also a statement of compliance as well as the relevant fee. Again, there is no set form of written agreement but the Limited Liability Partnership is obliged to keep a register of members and it must have a registered name which ends with "limited liability partnership" of "LLP".

CHAPTER THREE
PROPERTY AND THE USE OF
THE LAND CAPITAL ACCOUNT

It goes without saying that a farm needs land; there needs to be land, be it a barn, field or wood, in order to farm it. Yet that does not necessarily mean that the farming business has to own the land. The land could be rented by the farming business for a commercial rent, or an uncommercial rent for that matter, or it can be used by the partners in the business under licence. In other words, land can be held within the partnership structure or outside it and there are pros and cons to both options. From a practitioner's point of view the important point is to consider the options when a partnership is formed, when the circumstances of individual partner's change, when succession planning is under consideration, when there is development potential on part of the land and when the taxation landscape changes.

3.1 Land as partnership property

When it comes to considering whether land is part of the partnership or not then the provisions of section 20 of the Partnership Act, 1890 need to be considered. Section 20(1) defines partnership property as *"all property and rights and interests in property originally brought into the partnership stock or acquired, whether by purchase or otherwise, on account of the firm, or for the purposes and in the course of the partnership business"*. Property can therefore be brought in as capital by a partner and credited to their respective capital account. Often these accounts are called Land Capital Accounts to distinguish them from general capital accounts which perhaps reflect cash contributions or livestock and deadstock. If cash in the business is used to purchase further land than that too can be added to the Land Capital Accounts. In the past it is often the case for the land to be added to the general capital in the accounts but modern best practice is for the partnership accounts to separate out the land capital from the general capital. In many farming cases, the senior generation of partners will have larger capital accounts than the more junior members of the partnership whereas the general capital account may be more evenly divided reflecting the capital cash contribution each partner has made. The partnership's interest could be the freehold interest in the land or it could be the leasehold interest (a tenancy held as an asset of the partnership).

The amount credited to the Land Capital Account remains static as fluctuations in value would represent capital profits or losses for the firm each year. Therefore the figures in the accounts often do not reflect the true value of the land. It is only when there is a reorganisation of the partnership, a partner retires, a new partner is admitted or a partner dies are the values updated. Within the partnership agreement there should be provisions specifically relating to the Land Capital Account including the percentages of the land value attributable to each partner's Land Capital Account, how profits and losses on the land are to be dealt with, how is the land in future to be valued and reflected in any withdrawal of capital by a partner and maybe options by particular partners to withdraw some of the land out of the partnership at a future date without the need for consent by all of the other partners.

3.2   The historic problem of land in partnerships

Farming Partnerships can last for many years and during that time facts become blurred. Land could have been held outside of the partnership and used by the partnership at its commencement, then perhaps at some point the advisors suggested bringing the land into the business and to record it on the balance sheet. Perhaps later still, further land is purchased using partnership money and maybe the odd field has been sold. Often you have a total muddle with vague and inconsistent records. Take the example of Tim, Malcolm and John. Three brothers who had inherited the family arable farm in the mid 1960s. At the time John was still a minor and so the title deeds just had Tim and Malcolm on the title. When John attained his majority nobody felt it was important enough to update the title deeds. Afterall the intention was clear; Tim and Malcolm held the land for all three brothers who farmed the land in partnership. Sometime during the 1970s the accountants advised the brothers to put the land into the business and the value at the time was reflected on their capital accounts. Even though the value of the land changed over the next thirty years the value in the accounts did not. Further cash was added by one partner and that amount was simply added to the figure in the capital account. An outlying field was sold and the cash used to upgrade the buildings on the land. Sadly, in the late 1990s Tim died and in the 2010s John passed away. There was no written partnership agreement and the surviving brother (then in his mid 80s) couldn't remember what had been agreed on the division of the farm. Unfortunately this is not an uncommon set of facts and the uncertainty of division coupled with conflicting family interests can lead to a toxic and often litigious outcome.

When faced with facts such as the above and, as we shall see in this chapter, there are a number of areas to consider:

- The title deeds – who are recorded as the legal owners of the land and how was the land acquired;

- The declaration of trust – is there a separate declaration of trust recording the beneficial interests of the land;

- The partnership agreement itself;

- The partnership accounts;

- Testamentary documents of the partners including the Wills and ideally a copy of the solicitor's file when the Will was drawn up in order to establish the intentions and understanding of the deceased partners; and

- The conduct of the partners and their professional advisors' understanding.

A further problem often encountered by professional advisors is getting the clients to understand quite complex legal points. From their point of view, they owned the land in their names, the accountant or lawyer has advised often for good tax or succession planning reasons to bring their freehold or leasehold interests in the land onto the balance sheet and, to that end, they sign a new partnership agreement. Other than a little more paperwork and the accounts containing an historic figure for the value of the land, very little has changed. Surely they can still do what they like on the land? It can be quite difficult but important to explain to clients their fiduciary duties as bare trustees, their obligations and duties to their fellow partners and the fact they no longer own the land directly but only have a right and interest in the capital of the partnership business.

3.3   Land used by the partnership but held outside it

Just because a partnership uses land to make a profit does not necessarily mean that this land is partnership property itself. This would be the case even if the land is co-owned and all the co-owners are partners in the farming business. Even though the profits generated from the land and the expenses incurred were met by the partnership, this is insufficient to change the status of the land. The land remains outside of the partnership and belongs to the partners as co-owners in exactly the same way as if there was no partnership at all. It is also perfectly possible for the land to be owned in different shares to those in which the profits of the partnership are shared. The two do not have to mirror themselves. Again, look at the terms of the partnership agreement. In the case of *Eardley v Broad (1970) 215 E.G. 823* the farming partnership agreement stated that the capital was to consist of the stock, machinery and other assets of the farming business but made no mention of the lease of the premises from which the business was being run. It was held that the lease remained outside of the partnership even though the rent had been paid by the partnership and the property was indispensable to the farming business.

It is generally assumed that the mere use of property is insufficient for it to be regarded as partnership property. But there are instances where the land is treated almost as an accessory to the trade and in these cases it has been found that the land is partnership property. For example, in the case of *Waterer v Waterer (1872) 15 Eq 402* the land used in a nursery business was held to be partnership property because of the nature of the business. The rationale behind this was that the growing of plant and tree stock could not be separated from the land itself as they needed to grow in the land. Could this same line of thinking be used in all arable farms? It would be hard to see the difference with growing a shrub in a nursery to growing winter barley in a field. However, in all probability the case of *Waterer v Waterer* can be distinguished because on the facts further land was purchased from the son's father's estate and with money also raised by way of mortgage from the nursery land and therefore by analogy the statutory presumption that the land was partnership property applied to all of the land not just the additional land purchased.

This would follow the reasoning in the more modern case of *Ham v Bell and others (2016) EWHC 1791 (Ch)* where the farmland had been made available rent free for the partnership's use and the partnership had met from time to time the costs of improvements to the land. But the judge accepted the proposition that, even so, this does not necessarily imply that the farm on which the crops grow is an asset of the farming partnership.

3.4 Licence

The case of *Ham v Bell and others (2016) EWHC 1791 (Ch)* demonstrates factors which are common in a lot of farming partnership cases; that of a licence to occupy. The land is held outside of the partnership perhaps by one or two co-owners who are also partners in the farming business. By the mere fact that they are partners they allow the partnership to occupy the land they own under licence. It is a purely personal relationship between the co-owner of the land and the partners in the business and, as such, can end at any time. In other words there is no security of tenure by the farming business. A particularly important point if the co-owner of the land were to die when the licence would automatically terminate, leaving the partners at the whim of the personal representatives of the deceased co-owner or if there was a major falling out between the landowner and the other partners in the farming business. The knock on effects can be significant – how would the growing crops be harvested if there is no right to be on the land, how would such an immediate termination effect the Basic Payment Scheme entitlements or the rights to other subsidies and grants, new premises would also need to be found for machinery and the housing and feeding of animals.

With a licence to occupy arrangement it is sensible to ensure that areas of potential future dispute are resolved at the outset. Common areas where frictions can arise include who pays for the maintenance and repairs of buildings, what about any improvements to properties and who is responsible to ensure the occupation complies with the obligations towards good husbandry and cross-compliance requirements?

3.5 Licence arrangements for Limited Partners

As described in more detail in other chapters, a limited partner cannot take part in the day to day business activities of the partnership if he or she is to retain the limited liability status. The question has therefore arisen as to what would the nature of any licence the limited partner could grant to the partners of the Limited Partnership over the land. Can a licence even be granted if he or she is prohibited to be involved in the day to day business activities? The rationale as to why it is fine for a limited partner and landowner to grant a licence to his co-partners is by separating the business activities from those rights inherent in owning land. The Limited Partnership Act, 1907 does not prohibit exercising the rights over the land just taking part in the day to day business activities. As a landowner he is therefore able to grant a licence or a tenancy on whatever terms he wishes.

3.6 Lease arrangement

The alternative to a licence to occupy arrangement is for there to be a formal lease between the owners of the land and the partners in the farming business. If a lease is to be granted to a partnership consisting of more than four partners, then strictly it is only the four trustee partners who need to be a party to that lease. However, it is now good practice for the other partners to be joined in either as contractual tenants or as sureties for the partner's obligations under the terms of the lease. This ensures that the landlord has direct rights of action against all of the partners in the business.

A question has arisen as to whether a landowner can in fact let the land to a partnership of which he is also a partner. This is on the maxim that you cannot be both landowner and tenant. The question was considered in the case of *Rye v Rye (1962) AC 496* and it was decided that a landowner could not let to himself but the Court did not determine whether it was possible for a person to let a property to himself and others as partners in a partnership. Despite the uncertainty it is now generally accepted that it is possible for one partner to grant a tenancy over the land to a partnership of which he is also a partner. In this instance it would clearly make sense for the landowner and tenant to be separately represented and for that tenancy arrangement to the farming partnership to be in writing.

3.7 Agricultural Holdings Act Tenancy

For lease arrangements already in place it is important that you establish whether the tenancy is governed by the Agricultural Holdings Act, 1986 (an Agricultural Holding Act Tenancy) or the Agricultural Tenancies Act, 1995 (a Farm Business Tenancy) as the responsibilities, rights of parties and the tax treatment are different. It is perfectly possible for partners to be joint tenants of an Agricultural Holdings Act tenancy (AHA tenancy) and, as such, for the partnership to enjoy greater statutory protection including greater security of tenure through statutory restrictions on the operation of a landlord's notice to quit. They can therefore be quite beneficial for ensuring the longevity of a farming business operated through a farming partnership. In these cases, it is important to ensure that the partnership does not automatically dissolve by operation of law on the death or bankruptcy of a partner. That can only be done by use of a written partnership agreement which opts the partners out of the specific provisions within the Partnership Act, 1890.

A large number of AHA tenancies are oral where the precise terms are vague or uncertain. In these circumstances it is unlikely that a covenant restricting alienation would have been agreed and therefore the partners are entitled to assign the benefit of the tenancy to a company thus ensuring its security in perpetuity. To avoid this scenario, a well advised landowner would serve a notice on the tenant to initiate the procedure under section 6 of the Agricultural Holdings Act, 1986. This would prevent the assignment of the tenancy to a corporate entity.

The date the tenancy began will usually assist in determining whether the tenancy is an AHA tenancy or a Farm Business Tenancy (FBT). As a general rule if the tenant was entitled to possession:

- On or before 30 August 1995 and on the basis it meets the criteria under the Agricultural Holdings Act, 1986, it will be an AHA tenancy;

- On or after 1 September 1995 and on the basis it meets the criteria under the Agricultural Tenancies Act, 1995 it will be an FBT unless the tenancy falls within one of the exceptions in section 4 of the Agricultural Tenancies Act, 1995.

The exceptions preserve the AHA status of a tenancy where the tenant was entitled to possession on or after 1 September 1995 and qualifies as a succession tenancy under one of the circumstances laid down in section 4.

Under the Agricultural Holdings Act, 1986 there are a number of instances where it is necessary to serve notices and counter-notices as tenant to the landlord. When the landlord is also one of the tenants can the co-tenants compel the landowning tenant to join in on the service of the notice or counter-notice? If faced with this situation then it is possible for the non-landowning tenant to seek a court order to compel the co-operation of his co-tenants on the basis that both are trustees of land and so are governed by the provisions of the Trusts of Land and Appointment of Trustees Act, 1996.

If the partners are joint tenants then the death of one partner would not trigger the requirements to meet the succession provisions under the Agricultural Holdings Act, 1986. This is because the Case G notice in the legislation makes reference to the notice to quit being given to the person before death who was the sole (or sole surviving) tenant under the tenancy. Therefore the succession provisions can only apply on the death of the surviving joint tenant.

3.8 Assignment of an Agricultural Holdings Act Tenancy to a partnership

Assuming the Agricultural Holdings Act tenancy is in the names of individual partners and that the Agricultural Holdings Act tenancy is not freely assignable, it would not be possible for a newly admitted partner to be assigned the Agricultural Holdings Act tenancy unless such new partner was a "qualifying successor" on the retirement or death of the existing tenant partner. The landlord would need to give consent to such an arrangement. Take the example of William and John who had been farming together in partnership since 1980 under an agricultural tenancy. John's grandson Peter (the only member of the family interested in farming) now wishes to come into the partnership and as William and John are of a certain age this seems like a good idea. The problem is that whilst Peter could become a partner in the farming business he could not become a tenant of the Agricultural Holdings Act tenancy because he would not qualify as a successor under the legislation. It might be possible for William and John to assign their tenancy to Peter but only with the landlord's consent which he is unlikely to give without some financial inducement. In these circumstances it may be worth considering negotiating favourable terms with the landlord to enter into the Farm Business Tenancy regime with the tenants being William, John and Peter.

3.9 Landowner entering into partnership with non-landowning partner – use of a licence

Where a landowner enters into partnership with a non-landowning partner, no licence creating exclusive possession is given. This was established by the Court of Appeal in the case of *Harrison Broadley v Smith (1964) 1 WLR 464* and means that the non-landowning partner cannot claim that he has been given a licence which was capable of being converted into an Agricultural Holdings Act tenancy by virtue of section 2 of the Agricultural Holdings Act, 1986. The partnership agreement has the effect of giving the partners a non-exclusive licence to farm the land for the purposes of the business. In the case of *Harrison Broadley v Smith*, the widow entered into a partnership agreement with D, under which D had the powers of manager and farmed the land. The widow subsequently sold the farm to her son and terminated the partnership arrangement. Subsequently the son contracted to sell the property and served notices on D terminating his licence. It was held that D only had a licence because a person could not grant a licence to himself on the construction of section 2 of the Agricultural Holdings Act, 1948. In this respect a licence to occupy land for agricultural purposes meant a licence granted to a 3rd party who would, during the currency of the licence have a right of exclusive occupation. It could not operate where the licensor remained in lawful occupation of the land for the same purpose as the licensee.

This case was followed by the House of Lords decision in *Bahamas International Trust Co Ltd v Threadgold (1974) 3 All ER 881* and has led to landowners widely using this arrangement to avoid the security of tenure obligations under the Agricultural Holdings Act, 1986. However for this to apply the partnership agreement or the written licence must show that the intention is, and in fact granted, for the licence to be non-exclusive. For example, the licensor as partner retains the rights to carry on the agricultural activities and to continue to occupy the land in common with the rights of his co-partners and the partnership.

Whilst the principles of *Harrison Broadley v Smith (1964) 1 WLR 464* appear obscure, there can be a trap when there is no written partnership agreement and the land is being held under mere licence. It follows that the partnership could be brought to an end on the serving of a notice. However, relying on this case, HMRC argue that, until the partnership can be determined, the landowner does not have vacant possession. Under section 116(2)(a), Inheritance Tax Act, 1984, 100% Agricultural Property Relief might be denied. Nor will the extension of the period beyond 12 months under ESC F17 assist as that concession only relates to tenanted agricultural land, not land subject to a licence. The answer is to make sure there is a partnership agreement in place which gives the landowner the right to vacant possession within 12 months.

3.10 Farm Business Tenancy

For new tenancies and those started on or after 1 September 1995, the lease would be a Farm Business Tenancy governed by the Agricultural Tenancies Act, 1995. The parties have significant freedom to negotiate the terms of the tenancy and there are no security of tenure provisions. Certainly for new arrangements, it is advisable for the landowner to grant the partnership a Farm Business Tenancy to regulate the position and to ensure that the landowner receives 100% Agricultural Property Relief, provided the other conditions of the test are met. It should be noted that Stamp Duty Land Tax may be payable depending on the term of the lease and the amount of rent payable.

3.11 Terms of the tenancy arrangement

It is always best to have the terms in writing. When reviewing the partnership arrangement as well as checking what type of tenancy is in place, it is sensible also to make a note of:

- The nature and terms of the lease arrangement;
- Whether rent is being paid and how is that being recorded in the accounts;

- Whether there are opportunities for the rent to be reviewed and, if so, dates relevant notices have to be served;

- Whether Stamp Duty Land Tax is payable and when; and

- The availability of Agricultural Property Relief for the landowner and at what rate.

3.12 Continuance of the Lease on dissolution of the Partnership

As a partnership is not a legal entity in its own right it cannot hold legal title to the property. Therefore any lease has to be granted to individual partners. This can present two future problems. Firstly, if the partners who hold the lease retire or die without first assigning the lease or having the ability to assign the lease to the continuing partners and secondly, on dissolution of the partnership.

For those partners who are not tenants then it would be inferred that they have a non-exclusive licence to enter onto the land to carry on the partnership business. As these are contractual in nature then they may not be determinable during the continuance of the partnership if the termination would strike at the very heart of the partnership business. You cannot have a farming partnership without the land upon which to farm. It might be argued in these cases that the only effective way to terminate the licences would be to dissolve the partnership.

Unless the tenancy contains a break clause on a dissolution the tenancy would continue in the names of the tenant partners and, if the partnership agreement is silent on the point then any of the partners can insist all of the partnership assets are sold and the proceeds divided after all creditors have been paid. This may require the raising of funds by one partner to buy out and take on the lease from another (if permitted by the partnership agreement) and how, in this instance, would the lease be valued? Other questions might include can the lease be terminated early on the dissolution of the partnership, what about ongoing obligations by the tenant and how would improvements to the property be compensated and to whom? It would make sense to address these issues within the partnership agreement at the outset.

A further difficulty with effecting a dissolution is when the landowner has let the land to himself and another partner. In the case of *Lie v Mohile (2014) EWHC 3709 (Ch)* Mohile granted a tenancy to himself and the other partner, Lie, in order to carry on the doctors' practice. It was not possible for Mohile to exclude Lie from the premises because Mohile is deemed to have granted a licence to Lie to enter the property in order to conduct the purposes of the business. Even once the partnership is dissolved, the lease does not expire because the partnership business continues for the purposes of winding up. To put this principle in a farming context, if Tom owns arable land and lets it to himself and Mike to farm in partnership, even if Tom dissolves the partnership in May, Mike has the implied right to continue farming the land for the purposes of winding up until the crops have been harvested in late August.

3.13   Land owned by the partnership

One of the fundamentals of land law and the transfer of land is that any disposition has to be in writing. Section 2 of the Law of Property (Miscellaneous Provisions) Act, 1989 provides that *"a contract for the sale or other disposition of an interest in land can only be made in writing and only by incorporating all the terms which the parties have agreed in one document"*. Not a problem when there is a written partnership agreement which incorporates an appropriate declaration of trust or a separate declaration of trust or transfer where there is a clear indication that the land is owned by the partnership. But equally there can be a perfectly valid and working partnerships without the need to have a written partnership agreement. In those cases how (not infrequent in a farming context) if a partnership is established and there has been no transfer or declaration of trust can you say that the land can be owned by the partnership in the light of section 2 of the 1989 Act? On the basis that a partnership does exist, then it may be shown by parole evidence that its property consists of land. This proposition was first established in the case of *Forster v Hale (1800) 5 Ves.Jr. 308* and subsequently followed and developed in later cases. The line of thinking is that if premises are necessary for the purposes of the partnership then there is a constructive trust that the land is being held as partnership property by virtue of the operation of section 20(1) of the Partnership Act, 1890. However, the position is far from certain. Can a constructive trust even arise under section 20(1) of the Partnership Act, 1890 as noted in the case of *Horler v Rubin (2011) B.P.I.R 718*? There has also been little judicial comment on the application of section 2 of the Law of Property (Miscellaneous Provisions) Act, 1989 in relation to establishing land as partnership property. The case law relates to its precursors – section 4 of the Statute of Frauds 1677 and section 40 of the Law of Property Act, 1925. The need for a written partnership agreement to avoid this uncertainty cannot be over emphasised.

On the basis that section 2 of the Law of Property (Miscellaneous Provisions) Act, 1989 has been complied and the intention is for the landowner to transfer land into a partnership then this can be evidenced in three ways. The first option is by a formal transfer of the legal title to the land into the names of the partners by way of a Land Registry form. A TR1 if all of the land in a particular title is to be registered in the names of the partners or a TP1 if only part of the registered title is to be transferred. It is important to remember that in accordance with section 34 of the Law of Property Act, 1925 (as amended) and also section 34 of the Trustee Act, 1925 the legal title to any land can only be vested in four persons. Therefore if there are more than four partners then they will hold the land on trust for themselves and their fellow partners. As the partners are holding the land on trust for the partnership they are subject to the Trusts of Land and Appointment of Trustees Act, 1996. This means that the court will have a wide discretion to make orders relating to the exercise of trustee's functions.

The second option is for there to be a separate declaration of trust whereby the legal owners declare that they are holding the land on trust for the partnership and that it will constitute partnership property. Such a declaration will take effect under section 53(1)(b) or (c) of the Law of Property Act, 1925. The danger can be if the completed Declaration of

Trust gets separated from the Property Deeds or the Partnership Agreement and a subsequent action is taken at a future date which does not take into account the terms of the Declaration of Trust. This is particularly problematic if the land is unregistered or the trustees' interests have not been noted on the registered title.

The third option (and probably the most common) is for there to be a declaration by the landowners within the partnership agreement declaring the land which constitutes partnership property. To avoid any uncertainty in the future as to which land is held within the capital account of the partnership or held outside it but used by the partnership, it is desirable to specify within the partnership agreement or a partnership memorandum a clear description of the land, a plan and (if registered) the Land Registry title numbers.

3.14 Absence of agreement on what is partnership property

In the absence of a clear transfer and/or declaration as set out above, how do you assess whether land is partnership property or held outside the partnership but used by the partnership? The tests are different if new land has been purchased or acquired by the partnership from that of an existing holding over which the partnership has operated. The point has been nicely illustrated in the recent farming case of *Wilde v Wilde (2018) EWHC 2197 (Ch)* which concerned the dissolution of a farming partnership and whether the 100 acre dairy holding in Derbyshire (which had been in the same family for a number of generations) was partnership property or not. Before 1978, Ben Wilde had owned the farm. In that year he entered into partnership and whilst the partnership's composition changed over time the partnership continued until it was dissolved. There was no question as to whether the partnership existed (despite the fact there was no written partnership agreement) but did Ben transfer the land onto the balance sheet in 1978 or at any point thereafter? The leading authority on this is a case called *Miles v Clarke (1953) 1 WLR 537* where the parties carried on a photography business as partners at will. Again no written agreement but the partnership's accounts did include the value of the lease of the premises from which the business was run. The judge disregarded the accounts as evidence that the lease was partnership property concluding that no terms ought to be implied into the partnership agreement, except those which are absolutely necessary to give business efficacy to the relationship. Similar reasoning was also applied in the farming case of *Ham v Bell and others (2016) EWHC 1791 (Ch)* where farmland was made available for the use by the partnership. Whilst the partnership had met the cost of improvements of the land, the judge held that it was not necessary to imply that the farm on which the crops grew or animals are fed is an asset of the partnership. The farming partnership could continue and operate equally as well whether the land was held within the partnership or outside. The Courts are reluctant to imply land is partnership property without clear undisputable evidence that it is so.

3.15 Purchase of new land during the duration of the partnership

It is up to the partners to agree between themselves what assets are to be treated as partnership property. Consequently, when farmland is being purchased the question should be asked as to whether the acquisition should be regarded as partnership property or held by the partners and used by the partnership. The default provisions are contained in sections 20 and 21 of the Partnership Act, 1890 but as these rules cannot be applied in the face of contrary agreement, a written declaration on the treatment of the new land is beneficial. It also follows that if the partners so choose, land which was held as a partnership asset could be altered so that it was not and vice versa. The key here is agreement, and in the absence of such agreement, reference would need to be made to the partnership agreement for any provisions to cover this. To that end, it is not uncommon for a provision within the agreement which allows a partner to draw out of the partnership some of the land upon giving appropriate notice to the other partners.

As has already been discussed, the problems tend to be when there has been no past discussion or agreement on how the acquisition of land was to be treated and there is now disagreement between the partners (or their respective families) as to what had or had not been agreed. If faced with this then to rebut the statutory provisions under the Partnership Act, the key areas to consider are:

- the circumstances and reasons for the acquisition of the farmland;
- how was the acquisition financed and where were funds sourced from; and
- how have the partners subsequently treated the land? This would include particular reference to the annual partnership accounts and did each partner approve and sign them.

Land purchased by the Partnership

If the money used to purchase the land came from the partnership then just because that property is purchased by one of the partners in his own name doesn't mean the land belongs to that particular partner. This would be the case even if there were no specific declaration of trust specifying that the land was owned by the partnership. The presumption is that the land is being held on bare trusts by the partner whose name is on the title on behalf of the partnership. This presumption is laid out in section 21 of the Partnership Act, 1890 as follows "*unless the contrary intention appears, property bought with money belonging to the firm is deemed to have been bought on account of the firm*". Note that this presumption can be rebutted but there does need to be clear evidence for this to be the case and more than just because it was being held by one particular partner, such as the money had been lent by the partnership to the individual partner. The Scottish farming case of *Longmuir v Moffat and others (2009) CSIH 19, 2009 SC 329* concerned a farmer who had purchased adjoining land, already farmed in partnership, with money belonging to the business. The Court held that just because the land was purchased in the farmer's name does not necessarily mean the beneficial ownership was the same.

Land purchased by co-owners using the profits from the business

Suppose the land is held outside of the partnership but used by the partnership and profits were generated from that business. In such a case the presumption would be that the co-owners of the land intended to acquire the additional land in the same way as they hold the original land. In other words, outside of the partnership. Co-ownership of the land does not in itself determine that the land is an asset of the partnership, even if the profits from the business occupying the land are shared by the co-owners as partners. The argument goes that there would be no logical reasoning why the new farmland would be held differently from the rest. If the parties had intended something different then they would have said so. If, however, the sole purpose of the purchase is to facilitate the purposes of the partnership and was obtained in the course of that partnership business then the presumption may be rebutted. The acquisition of the land is an accessory to the trading business. A good example of this would be the case of *Morris v Barrett (1829) 3 Y & J 384* where the profits of the farming business was paid into a joint account. Further land was purchased by one of the partners using money from that account in order for it to be farmed with the original land. Even though the original land was held outside of the partnership the new farmland was held to be partnership property. Establishing the circumstances at the time of acquisition is key. Did all of the partners regard the acquisition as being made by and on behalf of the firm and how were any previous acquisitions dealt with?

3.16 Improvements to property

Careful accountancy is needed if partnership money is used to make improvements to the property when the land itself is owned by one of the partners but used by the partnership for the purposes of the business. Examples might include a new agricultural building being built on the land using partnership money or a new drainage system is installed on the farm. It would be wrong for the partner owning the land to be exclusively allowed to gain the benefit of the outlay made by the partnership. Any improved value of the property should be treated as a partnership asset and therefore that improved value element needs to be divided accordingly between the landowning partner and his/her co-partners as provided in the partnership agreement. In the case of *Pawsey v Armstrong (1881) 18 Ch D 698* it was held that whilst the leasehold interest in the Mills belonged to Mr Armstrong and held outside the partnership, the improvements to the property, which had been paid for out of the partnership profits, had increased the value of those properties. It was concluded that this increase in value was therefore, partnership property and would be divided accordingly in a dissolution of the partnership.

3.17 Execution of Deeds

For a deed to be validly executed by the partnership, it must be executed by all of the partners. It is only possible to delegate partner's functions including the operation of a power of attorney if it has been authorised in the partnership agreement signed by all the partners.

3.18 Limited Liability Partnerships

Unlike ordinary partnerships, Limited Liability Partnerships are able to own land directly. There is also no restriction equivalent to the Partnership Act, 1890 that the partnership property can only be used exclusively for the purposes of the partnership's business. There is, however, a duty for members to account for any profit derived from the property's use which is similar to the duty of partners under an ordinary partnership.

Any document does not need to be signed by all the partners. It is sufficient for the Limited Liability Partnerships to affix its common seal, or signed on behalf of the Limited Liability Partnerships either by two members or a single member and a witness. These provisions are contained in section 44 of the Companies Act, 2006 as applied by Regulation 4 of the LLP Regulations 2009.

CHAPTER FOUR
GENERAL CAPITAL AND FINANCE

Two partners come together and form a partnership. Whilst both have the intention to make a profit in their business their contributions of capital at the beginning was unequal. One of the partners could simply not afford to contribute a large amount of cash whilst the other could. Two and a half years later the business was sold. How should the capital be repaid? Should it be on the basis of what each partner introduced or on an equal basis? What if the amount to be repaid is higher than the sum originally introduced, should that "capital profit" be repaid in the same proportions or equally? These were the questions considered in the case of *Popat v Shonchhatra (1997) 3 All ER 800* which, whilst involving a news agency basis, could also apply in a farming context.

4.1   What is capital?

In the case of *Reed v Young (1984) STC 38 Nourse J* noted that "*the capital of a partnership is the aggregate contributions made by the partners*" and credited to them in the accounts of the business. The capital is what each partner has contributed, but to simplify matters to a straightforward financial transaction for farmers would be wrong. As well as a lifestyle choice, a prime motivation in becoming a partner is being part of the management and ownership of the business you are working for. It is not purely to contribute money to the business as an investment. This is particularly relevant for junior partners in a farming partnership. Their motivation in joining into the farming business is to make a contribution to the management of the farm, perhaps with new ideas and ways of working or proposals to diversify the core agricultural business. In a lot of cases they lack actual cash to invest but are prepared to make it up with enthusiasm and sweat. Often it is the senior established generation of partners who have already contributed, or are in a position to contribute, capital to the business.

Without a partnership agreement the principle of equality as set out in section 24(1) of the Partnership Act, 1890 applies. This states that "*all the partners are entitled to share equally in the capital and profits of the business*". So, in the above example, the junior partner would, without the certainty of an agreement, be entitled to the capital in equal shares to that of the senior generation. Consequently it is advisable for a partnership agreement to record how much is contributed by each partner in order to disapply the presumption contained in section 24(1).

The case of *Popat v Shonchhatra (1997) 3 All ER 800* drew a clear distinction between partnership capital and partnership assets (or property). The partnership capital is the amount each partner has agreed to contribute to the business. It is a fixed sum and based on hard cash contributed. It is a sum which does not increase or decrease without the consent of the other partners. Partnership assets, on the other hand, includes everything which belongs to the firm and consequently their values will vary from day to day. The value of the farming machinery belonging to the partnership will vary over time, the value of the original sum contributed by the partnership does not. There is a clear distinction between a partner's share of part of the capital of the partnership and his share in the assets of the partnership whose value is over and above the amount of the capital figure contributed. In other words, the capital profits and losses.

The capital accounts of a partnership cannot be varied without the agreement of all the partners. If further monies are contributed to a partnership by a partner they can only be credited to the capital account if all of the partners consent.

4.2   Interest on capital contributions

As the general capital of the partnership is the amount contributed by each of the partners, and is a fixed amount, is interest attributable to the amount invested? Section 24(4) of the Partnership Act, 1890, provides that a partner is not entitled "*to interest on the capital subscribed by him*". So as a general rule, interest is not charged on the amount invested but this rule is subject to any contrary intention by the partners, ideally recorded in the partnership agreement. This can be a useful device to distribute monies to the senior generation (on the assumption that they were the ones who contributed most of the capital cash) before net profits are ascertained. Bill, the father, due to his age and ill health, no longer works physically on the farm and as such it was felt in the family that the younger generation ought to receive a larger share of the net profits. Afterall it was their sweat and toil that produced the profit. Yet Bill had contributed most of the capital assets. The interest on the capital contributions is another way to slice up the profits prior to applying the profit-sharing ratio and may be more politic for the family then a prior share (like a salary). However, the income tax treatment is that the interest is treated as simply being an allocation of the profits of the business.

4.3 What is included in the general capital of a farming partnership

This is the amount each partner has contributed and is distinguished from the assets of the partnership. Invariably, the cash contributed has been spent. It is not just sitting in the partnership bank account. Often the money has gone towards purchasing machinery, livestock, fertilisers etc but on any dissolution, when the assets of the partnership are sold and turned back to cash, that cash is used to repay the capital introduced. Any surplus in the value of the assets of the partnership is deemed capital profits.

Often in farming partnership accounts, there is recorded the value of the deadstock and livestock on the balance sheet. As well as physical assets, it is probable that any government subsidies and entitlements are also included as partnership assets. The most common of which are the Higher Stewardship Schemes and the Basic Payment Scheme. The latter is the current main scheme for direct payments to farmers under the Common Agricultural Policy. This scheme replaced the Single Farm Payment Scheme on 1 January 2015. To be eligible, the partnership must have at least five entitlements; be a farmer during the year in question and claim against at least five eligible hectares.

On 16 January 2020 the government published the Agriculture Bill which is designed to replace the Common Agricultural Policy. The Bill sets out plans to phase out the current payments to farmers by 2027 and for it to be replaced with a new system geared more towards environmental land management. This change will have a significant impact on agricultural businesses and, in particular, those farming partnerships which rely on the payments in order to generate a profit each year.

As the entitlements were allocated largely on the basis of entitlement under the Single Farm Payment Scheme the values do not usually appear on the balance sheet of the partnership, though they can be an asset of the partnership. As the entitlements are personality rather than reality, they do not necessarily follow the land and they should be dealt with specifically in the partnership agreement.

The Basic Payment Scheme payments (paid annually) to the partnership will be treated as general income in the accounts. Any obligations for cross compliance are an obligation of the partnership to meet.

4.4 The assumption of equality

The starting point, in accordance with section 24(1) of the Partnership Act, 1890, is that each partner is entitled to the capital of the partnership in equal shares. So, Jack and Edward contributed £50,000 each to the partnership. Each will be entitled to that capital sum on the dissolution of the partnership.

More common in farming partnerships is for there to be an unequal contribution of capital introduced. In these cases it would seem unequitable for the partners to share the capital equally. The Courts have agreed with this approach and therefore if the partners have contributed unequally then that has been held as sufficient evidence to negate the presumption of equality. Having said that, unless specifically accounted for, it is quite possible for the partners to have agreed to negate the presumption of equality in their return of capital but not as to their right to share in capital profits.

Alex contributed £25,000 and Harry £75,000 of capital to a farming partnership. This was used to purchase livestock and deadstock the value of which totalled £200,000 when the partnership was dissolved some years later. Alex and Henry would receive back their capital contributions of £25,000 and £75,000 respectively. But what about the £100,000 of capital profit? Unless the presumption is rebutted, this capital profit would be divided equally which probably not what Alex and Harry would have expected. This is quite an important point to watch out for when there is development land being sold as again that capital profit could be regarded as being divided equally between all of the partners.

In the case of *Popat v Schonchhatra (1997) 3 All ER 800, CA* the two partners had contributed in unequal proportions. When the partnership business was dissolved two and a half years later, the Court of Appeal held that the original amount invested should be repaid in the same proportions as the provisions of section 24(1) had been ousted but that the capital profits should be divided equally. A good partnership agreement will provide for the division of capital profits as well as capital introduced but in the absence of such an agreement it will be a question of fact in each case to establish whether an express or implied agreement to vary the presumption has been made.

The other interesting point about the case of *Popat v Schonchhatra* is that the partners could agree to the unequal division of income profits or capital contributed but that does not necessarily mean that capital profits are also divided on an unequal basis. A dispute arose in the profit-sharing ratios of the band, The Smiths, (*Joyce v Morrissey (1998) TLR 707, CA*) and the question was whether the drummer, Mike Joyce, was an equal partner and entitled to 25% of the profits. The presumption of equality had not been displaced simply because Morrissey (and another band member) had done most of the work or that the continuance of the partnership had amounted to an acceptance of the change or that the accounts had been altered and not queried by Mike Joyce. None of these implied acceptance of a variation to the equality rule. Importantly there was no evidence that Mike Joyce had understood the significance of the accounts and the accountant had not specifically alerted him to the alteration.

4.5 Accounting treatment of undrawn profits

It can be the case that income profits remain in the business and not withdrawn in the accounting period in which they have arisen. There may be for a variety of reasons for this; the income is not needed by the partner; there is an intention to capitalise the sum and use the money to purchase additional assets or the money is simply left in the business to be withdrawn at a later date as a sort of savings plan. A particular difficulty arises if the accounts do not distinguish between the undrawn profits (a current account) and the fixed capital account. In other words, there is just one account invariably styled capital account. In these circumstances it is impossible to ascertain whether the partners had intended to capitalise the undrawn profits (the consent of all of the partners would be needed for this) or to treat them as simply undrawn profits to which a particular partner is able to drawdown at any point. In the farming partnership case of *Hopper v Hopper (2008) EWCA Civ 1417* the Court of Appeal upheld that the undrawn profits had been capitalised on the basis that the partners had, year on year, approved the accounts which treated the undrawn profits as capital. Yet the position remains unclear and it is far better to avoid the disputes by simply having separate current and capital accounts. If the partners agree that money in the current account can be capitalised then it is simply a debit/credit exercise to demonstrate the movement. A far more transparent method to deal with the issue. When professionals take on a new client with an existing farming partnership agreement, it is sensible to review the position and establish what is in the income account and capital account if not distinguished in the annual accounts.

4.6 Losses

Unless the partnership agreement says otherwise, the default rule would be that any losses are borne by the partners in the same proportions as the profits are shared. Like capital profits, this would be the case even if the contributions of capital were unequal. This rule can have unintended consequences for the partners. Richard, Harvey, Suzanne and Sarah farmed in partnership together. Richard and Suzanne had contributed most of the capital, £20,000 each. Harvey had contributed £10,000 and Sarah £5,000. On the dissolution of the partnership and the sale of the assets once all the creditors had been repaid there was only £43,000 left to repay the capital contributed. This would mean that subject to any contrary intention, each partner would bear the loss of £3,000 each. So, Richard and Suzanne receive £17,000 each, Harvey £7,000 and Sarah £2,000. If Sarah had invested nothing or the losses were more than £20,000 (£5,000 each) then she would be required to reimburse her co-partners for her share of the losses in excess of the capital she had contributed.

4.7 Loans to the Partnership

Monies contributed by an individual partner to the partnership do not necessarily have to be treated as a capital contribution requiring the consent of all the partners. It can be treated as a loan to the partnership. In which case the usual debtor/creditor relationship arises. Subject to contrary agreement, the partners may be paid interest on any loan at a fixed rate of 5% (section 24(3) of the Partnership Act, 1890). In the current climate this seems quite a high rate of interest and therefore it may be desirable to vary that rate by agreement either specified in the partnership agreement or in a separate loan agreement signed by all the partners.

Under the provisions of section 44 of the Partnership Act, 1890, loans made by the partners will rank ahead of capital contributions on a winding up of the partnership.

4.8 Partnership Books and Accounts

The Partnerships (Accounts) Regulations 2008 SI 2008/569 specify that a partnership must prepare annual accounts and obtain an auditor's report. These accounts should be made available at the partnership's principal place of business. For farming partnerships this should be the farmhouse and a provision to that effect should be placed in the partnership agreement. The reason being that it is helpful evidence to put to HMRC that the farmhouse is the place of business where the farmer lived when making a claim for Agricultural Property Relief on the farmhouse.

In accordance with section 24(9) of the Partnership Act, 1890, every partner has the right to inspect the partnership books, when he or she thinks fit and take a copy of any of them. This includes the right to use an agent to look at the accounts on that individual partner's behalf.

4.9 Limited Partnerships

The rules for limited partners are largely the same as for ordinary partners. However, the biggest difference is that limited partners, on the basis that they do not take part in the management of the firm, are only liable for losses to the extent of the capital introduced. So in the example in 4.7 above, Sarah would not need to reimburse her co-partners if the losses exceeded the amount of capital brought into the business.

The other major difference is that limited partners are unable to withdraw capital, and if it is withdrawn, the partner remains liable for the amount withdrawn. Often this means that it is preferable for limited partners to contribute monies by way of loan to the limited partnership, which are not affected by these rules, rather than capital introduced.

4.10 Limited Liability Partnerships

Regulation 7(1) of the LLP Regulations 2001, state that subject to contrary agreement, members share profits equally. Unlike ordinary partnerships, however, there are no default provisions for the sharing of losses. Like limited partners, a member is only liable to the extent of the capital within the partnership and not further or otherwise.

There is nothing in the legislation which makes provisions for interest on loans by members and so, if this has not been specified with the partnership agreement, no interest is payable on monies loaned by members to the Limited Liability Partnership.

Limited Liability Partnerships are subject to disclosure of their accounts and they must be prepared in accordance with the relevant legislation. The accounts of a farming Limited Liability Partnership will need to be audited and copies provided to all members as well as being filed at Companies House. Are the farming partners comfortable that their business accounts are in the public domain?

4.11 Rectification of farm partnership accounts

Care should be given to ensure that the farming accounts are firstly understood by the parties and the professionals and that they truly reflect what is happening on the ground. The risk of the clients and indeed the professional advisors, not understanding the accounts can mean that they are incorrect with regard to the interpretation of the ownership of the farm and, in these cases, it is important that the accounts are rectified. If on the preparation of the partnership agreement (or a review of its terms) which includes a forensic analysis on the legal ownership, this brings to light a discrepancy with the farm accounts then the accounts should be adjusted to reflect the correct position. In the case of *Ham v Bell and others (2016) EWHC 1791 (Ch)* the accounts had shown the farm as an asset of the partnership when it should not have done so for the period 1998 to 2003. The mistake was based on an assumption made by the accountants that there had been an agreement to make the farm a partnership asset. Yet there was no evidence of any discussion between the accountants and the Ham family about whether the farm had become a partnership asset. None of the accounts during this period had been signed in manuscript by the parties.

CHAPTER FIVE
DIVISION OF PROFITS AND LOSSES

It may not be the rationale to creating a farming partnership but there is always a hope that the farming business will at some point make a profit. This is not always an easy ask particularly in times where the Basic Payment Scheme is being withdrawn and farming margins are being squeezed. If the business is to make a profit then it is important for any partnership agreement to set out how those profits are to be divided. Conversely, for those businesses making losses the agreement needs to deal with how and who is required to contribute to those losses.

An interesting dimension for many family farming partnerships is the inter-generational partner element and how should the "sweat equity" of the more junior and perhaps more active partners in the business should be rewarded. It is often this generation with perhaps a young family to support which needs a guaranteed income. Take the example of Lower Town Farm, a farming business run by Tom Radford aged 78, together with his sons, Richard and Michael. Michael is really only a partner in name as he has a career elsewhere and does not take an active role in the day to day running of the farm. In the past Tom would have physically helped out on the farm, but he is now reaching that age when this is not practical. This leaves Richard, though whilst a junior member of the partnership is the one who is doing most of the physical work on the farm and is the one keeping the farm going. Tom needs the income to supplement his old age pension, Michael feels he is owed something from the farm and Richard feels he ought to get a share of the income profit to reflect the actual work he is doing. Not an uncommon situation, and one which needs to be addressed and reflected in the partnership agreement.

5.1 The presumption of equality for capital

As we have seen in chapter 4, Section 24(1) of the Partnership Act, 1890 states:

"All the partners are entitled to share equally in the capital and profits of the business, and must contribute equally towards the losses whether of capital or otherwise sustained by the firm".

This provision is predicated on the notion that it can be varied by express or implied agreement between the parties. That relates to both capital profits and income profits. It is perfectly possible for a partner to share in the profits and losses of an income nature and have no interest in the capital. The danger is that this may, however, give rise to disputes over whether expenditure is of a capital or income nature.

5.2 Right to a share of income profits

Every partner has the right to a share of the income profits. That is the net income after all the expenses of an income nature have been paid. A share of the profits is a normal incidence of being in partnership: it is the rationale for the partnership to exist in the first place. If the intention is not to make a profit and share those profits amongst the partners then there is no reason to create a partnership. That does not mean, of course, it has to make a profit year on year and making a profit is not a pre-requisite for its creation. Many farming partnerships do not make profits each year but when they do, the assumption is a division of those profits amongst the partners.

In order to calculate the income profits in any given year, you need to deduct the expenses made during that same period. There is a distinction, and also a potential area of dispute, between those expenses which are paid out of income (known as ordinary expenses) and those paid out of capital or borrowings (extraordinary expenses). Ordinary expenses in a farming partnership might typically include car expenses, fertiliser, seed, rent, insurance, fuel and administration costs for running the farm. Extraordinary expenses will typically be those one-off expenses such as the purchase of plant and machinery and expenses relating to improvements to partnership property. The decision process of whether an item of expenditure is income or capital in nature is a threefold process:

1. Generic – what is the nature of the expense and does it follow the ordinary nature of the trade being undertaken by the partnership;

2. Specific – is there anything within the partnership agreement or minutes of the partnership which specifically dictate how the expense should be dealt with; and

3. Consultation – using the working papers and in consultation with the accountant and the partners is it more beneficial from a taxation mitigation point of view to place the expense as income or capital? This would be subject to a contrary intention expressed in the partnership agreement.

If the partners cannot decide as to whether a particular expense ought to be treated as ordinary or extraordinary then the decision could be taken by a majority vote. This is because such a decision goes to the heart of the manner in which the business is to be conducted on a day to day basis. As such, it falls within section 24(8) of the Partnership Act, 1890 which states that "*any difference arising as to ordinary matters connected with the partnership business may be decided by a majority of the partners*".

5.3 Division of income profits

The partnership agreement should state the ratios in which the profits are to be shared between the partners. Usually the partnership agreement states the specific division of profits on day one as a default provision. This is necessary unless it has been agreed by the partners that the income profits can be divided equally between all of the partners. Ideally, this is followed by a proviso which says "or such division of income profits as the partners shall agree from time to time". The purpose of this proviso is to give the maximum amount of flexibility to the partners to vary their income divisions from year to year. Such decisions should be made in consultation with the accountant at the end of the relevant accounting period and will take into account the work undertaken by the various partners during the year, the working tax papers, the family dynamics and the tax position of the various partners.

So, at Lower Town Farm, Tom, Richard and Michael get together with the accountant to discuss the division of profits based on the draft accounts for the year. The default provision within their partnership agreement (drawn up in 2005) divides income profits as to 70% for Tom, 15% for Richard and 15% for Michael. However, at the time the partnership agreement was drawn up Tom was still very much physically involved in the running of the farm, Michael and Richard were still living at home and had a much less active role in the day to day farming business. Time has moved on, and to reflect that, the partners agreed that Tom's income share should be reduced to 35%, Michael remains at 15% and Richard, who is doing most of the physical work on the farm, has the remaining 50% of the income profits.

The above example is a fairly straightforward way to divide profits but it is not the only way. The partners may decide other ways to share profits including a "preferential share" to a specific partner before the residue is divided and interest payments for capital introduced and used in the business. Rather than Richard getting 50% of the profits, it may be decided that he should get the first £20,000 of profits and the balance divided into thirds for each to the partners.

These more complex arrangements can cause problems when assessing the amount of profits due to an outgoing partner on retirement or death. For example in the case of *Watson v Haggitt (1928) AC 127, PC* there were provisions for the payment of a preferential income share to a partner with the net residue divided equally between the three partners. On the death of one of the partners the agreement stated that the survivor was to pay the deceased partner's estate one third of the "net income profits". The question was whether that one third took into account the preferential income share payable to the continuing partner. The conclusion reached by the Privy Council was that no allowance could be made for the deduction. This was because the net profits in relation to a dissolution of the partnership did not have the same meaning as given to it whilst the partners were all alive.

As the decision on the quantum of income profits is "an *ordinary matter connected with the partnership business*" then it can be made by a majority vote of the partners in accordance with section 24(8) of the Partnership Act, 1890 unless, of course, there is a contrary provision within the partnership agreement. In the case of *Hammonds v Jones (2009) EWCA Civ 1400,* the issue was whether a former partner could challenge the accounts by which his share was to be ascertained. The partnership agreement provided that any disputes on the accounts would be decided by a majority of the partners and would be binding on all of the partners. The question was whether the quorum of partners included those partners who had retired from the partnership in the accounting period in question. The Court of Appeal concluded that it did.

5.4 Entitlement to withdraw

In the absence of an agreement by the partners or a provision within the partnership agreement, no partner will be entitled to withdraw his income profits until they have been ascertained at the end of the accounting year. For farming partnership and indeed for most partnerships this is unpractical. What does the partner live on in the interim period? It is therefore normal practice for the partnership agreement to authorise each partner to draw sums on account of the anticipated profit. This withdrawal would usually be subject to a reserve being made for tax and other partnership expenses. Like the establishment of the quantum of profits the timing of division (but not the manner in which the profits are to be shared) can be made by a majority vote of the partners.

5.5 Losses of an income nature

Like the treatment of capital losses, section 24 of the Partnership Act, 1890 states that in the absence of agreement, the losses are to be borne by the partners in equal shares. However, if the income profits are divisible in some other proportion as agreed in a partnership agreement then it assumed that the losses are divided in the same proportions. It is far better not to rely on an inference, and for the partnership agreement to state how losses of both a capital and income nature should be divided between the partners.

If one partner pays more than his share of the partnership debt, he will be entitled to reimbursement from his co-partners in order to correctly reflect the loss-sharing ratios.

5.6 Accounts and allocation of profits

The partnership accounts are prepared on similar lines to those of the accounts of a sole trader. So the general sequence of events is as follows:

- Separate general capital (perhaps land capital as well) and income/current accounts are updated for each partner;

- Any entitlements to preferential shares on division of profits to be debited or credited in the profit and loss account;

- Any interest on capital to be added; and

- The net trading profits and losses (after deduction of expenses) are then divided in accordance with the partnership agreement or by agreement of the partners.

CHAPTER SIX
MANAGEMENT AND DECISION MAKING

Most businesses of more than one person will have some sort of management process and a degree of delegation. A farming partnership is no different. Clearly for a partnership of two people, say husband and wife, the management process and delegation is fairly simple and happens as a matter of course without too much thought. Beyond that, however, particularly for a partnership with multi-generational interests, there is a need for thought, consideration and adoption within a partnership agreement.

6.1   Right to management

In default of any contrary provisions within a partnership agreement, the general provision is that every partner has the right to take part in the management of the business. Each partner has agreed to enter into business for their own mutual advantage and therefore they have the right to participate in the management and administration of the firm. The relevant provision within the Partnership Act, 1890 is section 24(5) which provides that *"every partner may take part in the management of the partnership business"*.

Any attempt to exclude a partner from the management of the business would invalidate any decisions taken in that respective partner's absence unless the partnership agreement stated otherwise. In the case of *Golstein v Bishop (2013) EWHC 881 (Ch)* one of the partners had attempted to make decisions contrary to the agreement and therefore in clear breach of it. But in practice, beyond a two-partner partnership, how practical is it for every partner to be involved in every decision of the partnership? Is each partner going to be actively involved in managing the livestock or deciding when to call the vet or deciding the day to fertilise the crops? Particularly problematic is when you have non-farming members of the family also as partners in the business. They are not going to want to engage on a daily, perhaps on an hourly, basis to make decisions and consequently some form of delegation of the management and the decision-making process has to be in place. Often the non-farming family partners will be located away from the farm and though they would wish to be consulted on big decisions, the day to day matters connected with the farming business will be of interest to them. It is therefore advisable to provide provisions within the agreement as to the management and decision-making limits of individual partners.

6.2 Management by "farming" partners

Where you do have partners who are more actively involved in the day to day farming activities it is possible, within the partnership agreement to agree that the right to manage some of the day to day affairs are conferred on them to the exclusion of those partners who are not actively involved on a day to day basis. In other words, the right to take a certain class of management decision without reference to the whole partnership. Take the example of a farm where you have three siblings, John, Thomas and Pippa in partnership together. Pippa lives in Leeds, eighty miles from the location of the farm. Thomas lives a little closer but not close enough to be on the farm every day. It is only John who lives on the farm and undertakes most of the farm labour. It is clearly not practical for Pippa and Thomas to be involved in all the day-to-day decisions on the farm. Therefore the partnership agreement specifically states that John has the authority to make decisions in relation to the day to day health and condition of livestock, the movement of animals, transportation to market and other decisions where the total liability of the partnership including invoices does not exceed £5,000. Decisions relating to the provisions of accountant services, improvements to farm buildings and purchase of new livestock and machinery require the consent of Pippa and Thomas as well as John.

6.3 Decision making process by a majority of partners

The above example works well if Pippa, Thomas and John are in agreement most of the time, but difficulties can arise, particularly if there is sibling rivalry and one-upmanship, if agreements cannot be reached on a regular basis. It is therefore possible for the Partnership Agreement to specify decisions which require a unanimous decision of all the parties and those where the agreement of a majority of the partners is sufficient. If it is agreed that certain decisions can be by majority then it should be clear whether weighted voting is appropriate perhaps in favour of the senior generation. This could assist and give comfort where there was a concern that the junior generation of partners may not be fit to run the business with a free rein or there were concerns about losing control too soon. Alternatives could be a simple majority vote or 75% of the votes are needed to pass the resolution. With different branches of the family being represented in the partnership a useful mechanism is for each branch to have a block of votes to reflect their particular interests. Say Pippa, Thomas and John having 50 votes each allocated to their respective families. Pippa has two children and decides to give them voting stock of 15 votes each, Thomas retains his 50 votes and John gives half of his votes to his wife. Under the terms of the partnership agreement a majority of 76 votes are needed to pass a specific resolution. One branch of the family cannot overrule the other two so it will require a combination of perhaps Pippa's children, John's wife and Thomas for the resolution to pass.

Subject to any express contrary provisions within the partnership agreement which alter the default provisions, not all decisions have to have unanimous agreement between the partners. Certain matters can be agreed by a majority of partners. The Partnership Act, 1890 separates those decisions where a majority agreement is sufficient, known as ordinary matters, and those decisions where a unanimous agreement is required. Section 24(8) of the Partnership Act, 1890 says "any difference arising as to ordinary matters connected with the partnership business may be decided by a majority of the partners".

Therefore decisions that relate to the manner in which the business is conducted on a day to day basis can be made by majority. Examples would include cropping rotas, fertilising, employing or dismissing seasonal staff, cutting hedges, maintenance of buildings, calling out the vet and repairs and maintenance of farm machinery.

6.4 Equal number of votes and deadlock

So, it is possible to deal with ordinary matters by a majority vote but if you have an even number of partners and there is no weighted voting, potentially it is possible to have a position where the votes are evenly divided. In such circumstances, the rule is in favour of maintaining the status quo. Taking this to its logical conclusion in a two-person partnership, one partner cannot unilaterally make decisions without the agreement of the other.

For partnerships with a larger number of partners there is often a provision for the managing partner (often the senior farmer in the family) to have the casting vote.

6.5 Rights of minority and acting in good faith

At the heart of a partnership is the obligation of each and every partner to act in good faith towards his or her co-partners in all partnership matters. This includes decisions taken by a majority of partners and is shown by conduct. Therefore it is a fundamental right for every partner to be fully canvassed and his or her views considered before any decision is made. If the decision then is to continue on a particular course of action and to do so would disadvantage the minority, (likely to be the dissenting partner) that is still a legitimate exercise of the power. This is on the basis that the decision was not made out of some improper motive such as victimisation or deliberately to disadvantage the minority partner.

6.6 Unanimous decisions

Unanimity is required to change the nature of the business as this is fundamental to the partnership. This is laid out in section 24(8) of the Partnership Act, 1890 which states that "*no change may be made in the nature of the partnership business without the consent of all existing partners*". In the context of farming the most obvious issue where this might arise would be over diversification of the core farming business. Many farming businesses need to diversify in order to survive, whether it is holiday lets or harvesting solar energy or developing redundant agricultural buildings into commercial offices. There has been little case law guidance on whether such diversification schemes would constitute a change in the nature of the business and so requires the consent of all of the partners. If the decision is being taken to commit the partners to a relationship and business activity which is fundamentally different to that when the partnership began, it is likely to require consent of all the partners. So, the question to ask on a diversification project is does the core activity of the business remain farming or has the nature of the business activity fundamentally shifted to something else? In any event, it would seem to be prudent move to obtain the consent of all the partners where there is an intent to diversify part of the business activities away from farming. Such a decision should be recorded in the partnership minutes. If the business plan at the commencement of a new partnership indicates that there are diversification plans in the near future, it would be sensible for these to be recorded in the new partnership agreement to accompany the new partnership.

Other fundamental decisions which require unanimity include the admission of a new partner. Section 24(7) of the Partnership Act, 1890 states that "*no person may be introduced as a partner without the consent of all existing partners*". This is common sense really as by the very nature of partnerships, the partners need to be able to get along and agree in order to run a business with a view to making a profit. Many partners do not like their co-partners but they are able to get along and, if they are unable to do so, the partnership becomes unworkable. As seen in Chapter 8, this provision does not prevent the assignment of a partnership interest to someone and that person can hold that interest and be entitled to profits from the business without being admitted as a partner.

The duty to vary the mutual rights and obligations of the partners under section 19 of the Partnership Act, 1890 also requires unanimity.

6.7 Delegation of management function

It is possible for partners to delegate their responsibilities under a power of attorney if authority to do so has been given in the Partnership Agreement. More detail on this is in Chapter 9.

6.8 Limited Partnerships

The whole point of Limited Partnerships is that some (but not all) of the partners have limited liability. In order to qualify for that limited liability, and in accordance with section 6(1) of the Limited Partnerships Act, 1907, those limited partners must not have a right to manage the partnership business. If they do, unintentionally become involved in the management of the firm then they will be personally liable for the partnership debts and obligations (like ordinary partners) during that period of management. That does not stop the limited partner inspecting the books nor examining the state and prospects of the partnership business, but they cannot be involved in the activity of management.

The obvious question is then, what constitutes management of the partnership business? In the case of *Inversiones Frieira SL and another v Colyzeo Investors II LLP and another (2011) EWHC 1762 (Ch)* it considered that participating in the decision-making process by commenting on individual decisions or scrutinising operational business decisions would constitute management of the partnership business. Passive activities such as inspecting the partnership books and expressing views about performance in general and commenting on strategy or future direction of the farming business would not.

Section 6(5)(a) of the Limited Partnerships Act, 1907 confirms that for making decisions on ordinary matters, it is only to be decided by the majority of general partners not all partners as for ordinary partnerships as governed by section 24(8) of the Partnership Act, 1890. This is common sense really, as to do otherwise, would mean that limited partners would be involved in the management of the business. This does not include (amongst others) variance of mutual rights and duties of the partners, the admission of new partners or the changing the nature of the business. All these require a unanimous decision of both limited and general partners.

6.9 Limited Liability Partnerships

Regulation 7(3) of the LLP Regulations, 2001 provides that all members have the right to manage and so, in this regard, Limited Liability Partnerships are aligned with ordinary partnerships. Ordinary matters are decided by a majority and it is only a change in business or an introduction of a new member which requires unanimous consent.

CHAPTER SEVEN
DEATH OF A FARMER

Nothing is as certain as death and taxes and that is no different in a partnership context. With an ever-ageing farming population and where the capital taxation system is such that you need to farm until you die there will inevitably come a time when a partner in the business dies. However, unless the correct documentation is in place, such as a decent partnership agreement which dovetails with the legal titles to properties and the partner's own Will, considerable problems can occur. It was this lack of robust documentation around the nature of the business and land holdings which was at the heart of the farming case of *Kingsley v Kingsley (2019) EWHC 1073 (Ch)*.

The case centred around the death of a partner in a farming partnership leaving his sister and co-partner at loggerheads with his widow. There were no promises between the powers and, crucially, no partnership agreement. Faced with such a situation, the question arose as to whether the sister could buy out the deceased partner's share in some of the farmland, without the relevant clauses you would expect to see in a partnership agreement, and, if so, at what price. Following Roger Kingsley's death in June 2015 the partnership had automatically dissolved. As there was no signed partnership agreement, only an undated draft from 1981, questions arose as to the extent of the individual partner's interests in the partnership, the extent of the beneficial ownership in the land and whether it was partnership property or not. All questions which could have been avoided if the appropriate written documentation had been in place.

7.1   Statutory presumption on death of a Partner

The presumption on the death of a partner is stated in section 33(1) of the Partnership Act, 1890 as being *"subject to any agreement between the partners every partnership is dissolved as regards all the partners by the death ..... of any partner"*. Potentially this could have significant consequences for the operation of the business and therefore to avoid the presumption of dissolution, it is advised that the partnership agreement contains a provision that dissolution of the firm will not take place on the death of one of the partners. The rationale behind this provision is simple in that it is no longer possible for the partners to adhere to the original agreement because one of them is dead and the essence of the agreement is that all of the partners are alive. The rule is strictly applied regardless of whether the partnership is for a fixed term or not and applies even in Scotland, where a partnership is afforded a separate legal personality. For the purposes of accounting, the date of dissolution is the date of death of the partner.

So, in the case of *Kingsley v Kingsley (2019) EWHC 1073 (Ch)* where there was no partnership agreement or contrary intention to rebut the presumption in section 33(1) of the Partnership Act, 1890, the death of Roger Kingsley was sufficient to automatically dissolve immediately the partnership and the consequences that flowed from that. The partnership bank account is frozen and that can be problematic particularly where there are farm employees who need paying. Who is going to pay for milking the cows until the Grant of Probate has been obtained?

7.2 Position of a sole surviving partner

If, on the death of a partner, there remains one sole surviving partner then the partnership can no longer continue and has to be treated as being dissolved, irrespective of anything to the contrary within the partnership agreement. The whole rationale of a partnership is that it exists between more than one person and so if there is only one person, the business can only continue as a sole trade. However, this does not affect the contractual rights the sole surviving partner may have to acquire the partnership assets, as set out in the partnership agreement.

The problem in *Kingsley v Kingsley (2019) EWHC 1073 (Ch)* was that the sister and sole surviving partner, Sally, had wrongly assumed, there was a contractual right for the sole surviving partner to acquire the partnership assets as such a right had not been recorded in writing. As in this case, where there is friction and mistrust between the executor (the widow Karim) and the surviving partner, this can present further complications. Karim, as executor, does not have the right to interfere with the dissolution of the partnership (that is the responsibility and right of the surviving partners) and whilst Sally tried to reassure her that she was aware of the need to ensure that the deceased's estate received the full value for its interest in the partnership and in the farmland, this was not believed by Karim. In this case, the Court held that Sally had acted properly and as required by the Partnership Act, 1890.

7.3 Personal Representatives becoming partners in the Business

Unless all the surviving partners agree otherwise, the personal representatives have no rights to be admitted to the partnership in place of the deceased partner nor are they permitted to interfere with the operation of the farming business. This is the same principle as the admission of any other partner in accordance with section 24(7) of the Partnership Act, 1890 in that unanimous consent is required. So there is little danger, without consent of the surviving partners, for the deceased's widow/widower to become a partner and interfering with the family business, but this needs to be balanced with the personal representatives duty to account for the estate and if no agreement can be reached, then the personal representatives are quite entitled to apply for an order for the business to be wound up.

It is not uncommon for siblings to be in partnership and to co-exist as such for many years but the extra dynamic of bringing in the widow or widower could prove the partnership's undoing. Take the example of Peter, Mike and Barbara. They happily farmed in partnership since the 1960s with no significant disagreements. Mike dies and his wife Sally wants to step into Mike's shoes and to continue the partnership. Whilst Peter and Barbara tolerate Sally there is no way they would want to go into partnership with her. There is a big difference between making polite conversation with Sally occasionally over Sunday lunch and being in partnership with her. It is not always easy for the professional to tease out these family dynamics when taking instructions on the partnership agreement unless there is a longstanding professional relationship but it is worth the time in the long run. Where there are apparent it is wise for them to be addressed within the partnership agreement by provisions to state that spouses of partners are unable to join the partnership. As much as Sally may not like it, the surviving partners are able to point to the provision, shrug their shoulders and comment that this was the agreement her late husband had signed.

It is, of course, possible for the personal representatives of the deceased partner to be admitted as partners (with the surviving partners' blessing) within the existing business but they are under no obligation to do so. It would certainly not be advisable for them to make that decision until they have been provided with details of the state of the partnership and have seen sets of accounts for the proceeding few years. Even if the personal representatives are comfortable with being admitted as partners in the farming business, if the personal representatives are professional advisors or the personal representatives are not actively involved with the day to day farming operation, then a limited partnership may be more appropriate.

If the intention is for the personal representatives, as trustees, to become involved in running the business then it is important that the Will contains the appropriate powers including an express power to trade. The statutory powers are restrictive and in essence allows the personal representatives to trade until such time as is necessary to sell the business as a going concern. A reasonable time would normally be regarded as not very much more than a year after the death (*Re Crowther (1895) 2 Ch 56*). If there is no express power to trade then it can be implied, if the personal representatives have been given a power, to postpone the sale of the business. This is because it can be presumed that if the power to sale has been postponed then that must mean the testator intended for the personal representatives to carry on the business.

If you are faced with an intestate situation, then in accordance with section 33 of the Administration of Estates Act, 1925 the administrators have the power to postpone the sale of the business for as long as is necessary in order to sell it as a going concern.

This is another good reason why it is so important that if you are putting in place a new farm partnership then it would be sensible also to review the Wills at the same time. Most modern Wills will incorporate in them the Society of Trust and Estate Practitioners (2nd Edition) Standard Provisions which includes a power to allow the trustees to "*carry on a trade, in any part of the world, alone or in partnership*".

7.4   Technical dissolution

It is, of course, much easier to value the relevant deceased partner's share and provide some method of sorting out the withdrawal or redistribution of that partner's share, whilst preserving and continuing the farming business as opposed to a general dissolution of the partnership. Where, in practice the surviving partners simply carry on the farming business, albeit by way of a new partnership immediately after the death of a partner, this is termed a "technical dissolution". Even a technical dissolution can have a significant impact, particularly in relation to secured borrowings and bank accounts. There has still been a dissolution and the terms and conditions of the Bank will give them an opportunity to renegotiate terms. This will be of particular importance if the terms previously negotiated were more favourable to the business than to the Bank. Those teams within the Banks who deal with farming businesses on a regular basis are usually flexible and understanding enough to simply amend the bank account details in accordance with the "new" partnership. If, and sadly it does happen, the farming business account is being dealt with by less understanding banking staff, the change in the partnership can lead to further complexity and anxiety whilst the bank account is frozen and potentially a new bank account has to be opened.

7.5   General dissolution

If there is no partnership agreement, the agreement does not exclude the provisions of section 33(1) of the Partnership Act, 1890 or a new partnership is not immediately formed then there is a general dissolution and consequently a winding up of the business. If a general dissolution occurs the partners have authority under section 38 of the Partnership Act, 1890 to carry on the business for the provisions of winding up only. In the case of *Hopper v Hopper (2008) EWCA Civ 1417*, Robert Hopper and his wife, June ran a farming business with their son Robert and his wife Lynn. There was no written partnership agreement and so on Robert senior's death in 2003, the partnership dissolved. Not realising that the partnership had terminated, Robert junior simply continued the business simply because he regarded it as his to continue. June Hopper argued that a new partnership had been created between herself, Robert junior and Lynn. The Court of Appeal held that there was no intention to create new contractual relations and therefore there was no new partnership. Robert junior's authority went only as far as section 38 allowed which was to do whatever is necessary to complete the outstanding transactions and to wind up the partnership.

During that time, when the farming business is being wound up, the personal representatives of the deceased partner do not have any authority to interfere with the business or the winding up of the business. That prerogative remains with the surviving partners. In the case of *Kingsley v Kingsley (2019) EWHC 1073 (Ch)* the widow could not interfere with the partnership business despite her misgivings on the way it was being handled by her deceased husband's sister, who was the surviving co-partner. That responsibility lay with the sole surviving partner.

7.6 The nature of the deceased's partner's interest

Where the partnership continues by the surviving partners then section 43 of the Partnership Act, 1890 provides that the amount due to the estate of the deceased partner in respect of his partnership share is treated as a debt accruing as at the date of his death. This is the case even though it will not, of course, be possible to ascertain the exact value of the debt until quite some time after the death. Valuations of the partnership property will need to be undertaken and agreed as well as finalisation of the partnership accounts up to the date of death. The importance of the deceased's partner's share being regarded as a debt in this instance is that the statute of limitations will apply, which means that after six years any claim will be statute barred.

As this is treated as a debt as at the date of death of the partner then the amount owed is static. It is fixed to that moment in time. It does not fluctuate as inevitably the value of the partnership property will from the date of death until the date the amount owed is settled.

Alistair died on 29 September 2018 but it took until October 2019 to obtain the valuations and finalise the accounts of the partnership up until that date. Alistair's share was valued at £750,000. However, during the intervening thirteen months the value of agricultural land had increased from £10,000 an acre to £15,000 an acre meaning that, had Alistair survived, his share would be worth closer to £1 million. The partnership had continued during this period and had benefited from the uplift in value. On the face of it that does seem unfair on the beneficiaries of Alistair's estate. To keep matters equitable, the provisions of section 42 of the Partnership Act, 1890 come into play to compensate Alistair's estate. See section 7.9 below.

7.7 Sale of the deceased's share to the surviving partners

Generally, there is no bar for the personal representatives to sell the deceased's partner's share to the surviving partners. Often in well drafted partnership agreements this is recorded by an option for them to do so. An option to purchase is often the preferred method rather than a binding obligation on the personal representatives to sell and an obligation on the surviving partners to purchase which would result in denying the availability of Business Property Relief from Inheritance tax as constituting an existing contract for sale. The option provisions within the partnership agreement should specify timing of the option period, the method of payment i.e lump sum or instalments and the method of valuation of the outgoing partner's share.

In relation to the timing of when the option can be granted, it is helpful to think about the practicalities and what needs to be established during that period. Often the option period is quite short, perhaps three or six months after the date of death. How practical in farming partnerships is that? If the land is held on the land capital account of the partnership it needs to be valued, as do the other assets of the partnership. All debts and liabilities arising up to the date of death have to be ascertained and accounts need to be prepared up to the date of death and agreed by the continuing partners. It may be very unwise for the continuing partners to offer to purchase the deceased's partner's share without knowing first what value is being placed on the deceased partner's share and consequently the price to be paid. Inevitably, a short notice period will place additional stress on the partners and professionals to establish a price in a tight timescale.

Thought also needs to be given to whether the payment should be made in one lump sum or in instalments with an appropriate rate of interest. This may depend on what the partnership assets are and the value of the share. If they include land then, in view of the value of agricultural land, it is likely that the value will be significant whereas if the partnership property is just the livestock the value may be lower. If the value of the deceased's partner's share is high, how is that going to be paid for? Will the continuing partners need to take out a mortgage? How does the payment out of the business affect cash flow? If there is a proviso for instalments within the relevant clauses of the partnership agreement, then how many should there be and over what time period? Often these will be annual payments over three, five or ten years. It is also wise to include, within the partnership agreement, the rate of interest to be charged on the outstanding payments.

The Court of Appeal decision of *Ham v Ham (2013) EWCA Civ 1301* demonstrated the importance of ensuring that the appropriate valuation provisions are within the partnership agreement and that the partners understand the implications of them. This case concerned a 178-hectare dairy farm in Frome, Somerset in which the partners consisted of Ron and Jean Ham (husband and wife) and their son, John. The business had begun in 1966 and John joined the partnership in 1997. The hope and intention of the parents was for John to one day inherit the farm and carry on the business. At first everyone worked well together, but by 2009 it was clear that there were material differences on the strategy of the future of the farm. John wanted to drive the farm in one direction, his parents disagreed and refused to relinquish control. As a result John resigned from the partnership citing irreconcilable differences with his parents. Under the terms of the Partnership Agreement, the remaining partners had an option to purchase the outgoing partner's share. The question and difficulty in this particular case was the value to be assigned to that partner's share. The written partnership agreement was poorly worded using the unhelpful phrase of "net value" to be agreed between the partners and, in default of agreement, by the accountants acting as experts. Ron and Jean Ham claimed that the value should be assessed on the book value of the assets as recorded in the accounts. A rather low amount as it did not take into account the rise in property values over the preceding ten years. John argued that it was the open market value of the assets at the time of his resignation. The Court of Appeal agreed with John's interpretation on the facts of the case that the open market value should be used and not the historic costs as his parent's understood.

Generally there are three options open to the partners:

- The historic value – shown in the accounts and which is unlikely to have been updated for many years. Consequently it is likely to be a low value and will have no reflection on the current value of the assets;

- Open market value – often the most used in modern agreements. In the probate context you will need an open market value in accordance with section 160 of the Inheritance Tax Act, 1984 anyway so you may feel that is a good and fair reference point to use; and

- Agricultural value – in other words the value of the property if used solely for agricultural purposes and not taking into account any additional value which could be hope or amenity value.

Very rare to see this option in practice and it does present questions on the values to be placed on the main farmhouse, farm cottages or areas made over to a diversified non-farming business. However, it is an option nevertheless.

Whichever option is selected it is also beneficial to provide for disagreements in the valuations between the personal representatives and the surviving properties by using an ultimate arbitrator.

A further problem exists when there is no option arrangement in writing. It is so important that the intentions of the parties are recorded and, where appropriate, to take the necessary instructions. As we have already seen in the case of *Kingsley v Kingsley (2019) EWHC 1073 (Ch)* the problem was the lack the documentary evidence and the basis on which any interests are to be valued.

One further point to watch out for is the potential for conflicts of interest issues to arise. Particularly important when the personal representatives are also the surviving partners. It would be appropriate in such a case to strongly remind the clients of their fiduciary duties as both personal representatives and partners in partnership and, where appropriate, making arrangements for independent persons to be appointed as trustees of the Will Trust.

7.8 Use of life assurance

A solution to give some available cash for the remaining partners to purchase the deceased's partners share is the use of life assurance. In other words, each partner takes out a life assurance policy on his/her own life which is then assigned into trust for the benefit of the remaining partners. The premiums would be paid from the partnership income account. In other words, before partners' drawings. In the event of the partner's death the policy proceeds would be made available to the trust's beneficiaries (the surviving partners) free of inheritance tax. It is helpful for the trustees to have the power in the trust deed that is holding the life assurance policy to have the flexibility for the monies to pass to the surviving partners in the same proportions as they hold their capital interests at the time of the death of the respective partner. This will then take into account changes in the partnership structure, from the taking out of the policy until the death of the partner, including taking into account the admission of new partners and the retirement of old.

7.9 Post dissolution profits and section 42 of the Partnership Act, 1890

As we have already seen, the deceased partner's share is ascertained and valued as at the date of death and is a debt owed to the estate of the deceased. The question then arises as to how profits should be dealt with from that moment until the continuing partners have repaid the debt to the estate. This could be quite some time as not only do valuations need to be completed but also the accounts finalised up to the date of death. It would perhaps be prudent for the executors to wait until the grant of probate had been obtained before paying out any monies.

If the surviving partners do carry on the farming business without final settlement of the accounts then, in accordance with section 42 of the Partnership Act, 1890, the estate of the deceased partner is entitled to either a share of the profits attributable to the deceased partner's share or interest at the rate five per cent on the amount of the deceased's share of the partnership assets. Section 42 only applies to an "outgoing partner" situation and not a full winding up and dissolution of the partnership. In the case of *Hopper v Hopper (2008) EWCA Civ 1417* one of the questions which arose was what was June Hopper's entitlement to post-death profits from the farming business? There had been a technical dissolution on the death of Robert Hopper senior and the business had carried on under the terms of a new partnership by the son and daughter-in-law only. There was no evidence of an intention to fully wind up the business or that June Hopper had become a partner in the new partnership business. Therefore, section 42 applied. The same would also apply in a retirement situation. In the case of *Truong v Lam (2009) WASCA 217* the retiring partner had agreed that he would only receive the price of his share and consequently he was entitled to elect that section 42 applied until final settlement of his interest.

The personal representatives of the deceased partner have a choice to make and that can only be made once they have undertaken the appropriate due diligence. They have a fiduciary duty to act in the best interests of the beneficiaries of the deceased's partner's estate and that may conflict with the interests of the continuing partners.

A share of the profits attributable to the deceased partner's share

When considering the share of profits it should be noted that this is income profits not capital profits. Capital profits are dealt with in accordance with section 24(1) of the Partnership Act, 1890 and potentially this will be on an equal split unless the presumption has been displaced expressly in the partnership agreement or impliedly by the actions of the partners. In the farming case of *Emerson v Emerson (2004) 1 BCLC 575, CA* one of the partners died in 1998 and the business had continued by the surviving partner. Compensation was paid for the slaughter of animals following the Foot and Mouth outbreak in 2001 and the Court of Appeal held that the monies paid should be divided in accordance with section 24(1) and not section 42. It does, however, apply to income profits and these are to be divided with reference to the use of the deceased partner's share of the assets and not to any previous income profit sharing agreement either expressly made in a partnership agreement or implied through conduct. This is quite an important point in many multi-generational farming partnerships where the income profit sharing ratios pre death are not the same as the capital profit sharing ratios. Often the senior generation will have a greater share of the capital profits (particularly land capital) whilst the younger generation may take a greater share of the income profits, perhaps to reflect the amount of daily physical labour he or she undertakes on the farm.

As the income profit sharing ratios post death are not the same as the income profit sharing ratios pre death then two questions arise when ascertaining what that sharing ratio should be. Firstly, as the amount is ascertained with reference to the respective interests in assets of the business, is that the gross value of the assets or the net value? In other words, after deduction of any liabilities of the partnership. The position is not entirely clear but the Court of Appeal in *Sandhu v Gill (2006) Ch 466* came to the conclusion that it is the net value which should be used. Secondly, should an allowance be made for the management of the business by the remaining partners? This will be a question of fact but it might be possible for the continuing partners to show that the profits were earned wholly or partly by other means than just the utilisation of the partnership assets. After all the continuing partners will still need to maintain and feed the cows in a Dairy herd or prepare the land in order to plant the winter barley.

Interest at the rate five per cent on the amount of the deceased's share of the partnership assets

Note that this option relates to a share in the partnership assets as distinct from the capital. In an age of low interest rates, a rate of 5% seems quite good and that rate, despite petitions to the contrary, has not changed since 1890. Many personal representatives faced with the option of applying section 42, with the background of low interest rates and challenging times to make a decent profit, may on the face of it choose this option. In the case of *Barclays Bank Trust Co Ltd v Bluff (1982) Ch 172* a farming partnership had continued between father and son until the death of the father in 1972. The son then started negotiating with Barclays Bank (who were the executors of his father's estate) to purchase his deceased's father's share of the partnership. The farm had increased dramatically in value during the years that followed and Barclays wanted clarification on whether it would still be entitled to an increase in the value of the assets between dissolution and the final account if it elected also for the interest at five per cent option. The Court held that the executors' rights to elect the five per cent interest option (instead of a share of profits) had no effect on the executor's rights to a share in the increased value of the assets. Section 42(1) only applies to income profits and not capital profits which are subject to section 24(1) of the Partnership Act, 1890.

A notice to elect for either option under section 42(1) must be clear and unambiguous to be effective. It should also only be done once the personal representatives have considered both options, have access to the relevant paperwork (including copies of the farm accounts) and have considered their fiduciary duties to the beneficiaries of the deceased's partner's estate.

7.10 Valuation of the outgoing deceased Partner's share

The starting point on any question of value of a deceased's interest in something for inheritance tax purposes is section 160 of the Inheritance Tax Act, 1984 which states that the value is "*the price which the property might reasonably be expected to fetch if sold in the open market at that time, but that the price shall not be assumed to be reduced on the ground that the whole property is to be placed on the market at one and the same time*". The way in which the partnership agreement deals with the deceased's partner's share may affect the value as a restriction on the deceased's right to dispose freely of his partnership share is taken into account for the valuation for inheritance tax purposes. However, this is only to the extent that consideration for money or money's worth has been given for it (section 163(1)(a) of the Inheritance Tax Act, 1984). If the restriction was not granted for full consideration then the open market value of the deceased's interest will be valued and taxable (subject to the availability of Agricultural Property Relief or Business Property Relief).

The actual valuation of the share will normally be by reference to the value of the underlying assets of the partnership. The significant value of agricultural land has highlighted the need to ensure that the partnership agreement has provisions within it to make it clear how the value of the assets of the partnership are to be assessed when calculating the net share of the deceased partner (ie the amount which will be paid to the estate of the deceased partner). There is no universally agreed formula for assessing that value but there are a number of methods which could be employed.

In the case of *Cruickshank v Sutherland (1922) 92 LJ Ch 136, HL* the partnership accounts had always shown the assets at book value. Under the terms of the partnership agreement on the death of a partner, the share had to be valued by reference to the accounts immediately before death. The House of Lords held that since the partnership agreement did not specify how a subsequent account should be prepared for the purpose of valuing an outgoing's partner's share and there was no precedent, the account should be prepared on the basis that the assets are valued at market value and not book value. The conclusion followed by the English Courts (the position is different in Scotland) is that each case will depend upon the construction of the partnership agreement and any course of dealings between the partners. So, in *Re White (2001) Ch 393, CA* the farm partnership accounts had always shown the assets at historic value and that value had been used when two previous partners had left the firm. The partnership agreement required that the outgoing partner should receive a just valuation of his share. Since all previous accounts used book values, using that method of valuation provided a just valuation for the purposes of the agreement.

In the case of *Drake v Harvey and others (2011) EWCA Civ 838* the Court of Appeal also held that there was no presumptive rule that market value, rather than historic value, should be used on the death of a partner. The method of valuation was to be determined by interpretation of the partnership agreement according to ordinary contractual principles. The farming partnership agreement provided that the deceased partner should be paid the amount standing to the partner's credit as recorded in the last set of accounts. Those accounts valued the assets at historic cost and not market value and the Court held that it was on this basis that the valuation should be set.

Whilst not itself relating to the death of a partner but rather a retirement, the farming partnership case of *Ham v Ham and another (2013) EWCA Civ 1301* considered the valuation point and the interpretation of the partnership agreement in relation to a dairy farm. The partnership agreement contained a provision that on serving a notice to dissolve the partnership by one of the partners, the other partners had the right to buy out the outgoing partner's share. The difficulty with the drafting was that the "net value" had not be defined with sufficient precision. The Court of Appeal ruled that there are no presumptions pointing towards a single basis of valuation. It is therefore necessary to take into account any relevant information in interpreting the partnership deed.

7.11 Valuation of Agricultural Holdings Act Tenancies

In the past, it was quite common for a landowner to let the farm on an agricultural tenancy to a partnership. In most cases the landowner was also a partner in the partnership business but occasionally not. Section 160, Inheritance Tax Act, 1984 refers to *"the price which the property might reasonably be expected to fetch if sold in the open market at that time"* but the difficulty with Agricultural Holdings Act Tenancies is that the tenancy is non-assignable in the marketplace. How then is it possible to value it as a landlord or as an interest in a farming partnership? Moreover if the landowner was also a majority owner of the business do the two interests merge as one to produce a higher value or are the interests separated for the purposes of the valuation? This very question was looked at in some detail in the case *of IRC v Gray (surviving executor of Lady Fox) (1994) STC 360* which concerned the valuation of various tenancies over a 3,000-acre estate. The estate was owned by Lady Fox and she had granted to herself, and two other partners, a tenancy over the land to farm the land in partnership. Under the terms of the partnership agreement, Lady Fox was entitled to 92.5% of the partnership profits. The question was do you arrive at the valuation of the tenancies through a hypothetical sale of the freehold reversion together with the leasehold interest (which would constitute a higher value) or value the freehold reversion and the leasehold interests separately (which would constitute a much lower value)? Due partly to the significant percentage of partnership profits due to Lady Fox, it was held that the two interests should be combined and valued as one.

The Lady Fox case was followed shortly by another, *Walton (executor of Walton) v IRC STC 68* which considered a similar point. In this case the farm was owned jointly by the father and his two sons. Again there

7. DEATH OF A FARMER • 81

as an Agricultural Holdings Act tenancy in favour of a partnership of which the partners were the father and just one of his sons. The partnership agreement stipulated that on the death of either partner, the survivor had the option to purchase the deceased partner's share. In this case, the deceased only had a one third interest in the freehold reversion and a half interest in the partnership. There was no majority holding. As the landowners had no intention of disturbing the tenancy as of fact the Court could not introduce into the hypothetical sale a hypothetical landowner who would bid more for the tenancy. The two interests had to be valued separately.

Whether a case falls under Gray or Walton will depend largely on the facts.

The following table sets out the more common situations that arise in a partnership context when valuing Agricultural Holdings Act tenancies:

Death of a Partner		
No interest in the freehold land		
Partner's interest in the Partnership	AHA tenancy not held on the Land Capital Account of the Partnership	The tenancy is not included in the valuation of the partner's interest in the partnership as it is not an asset of the partnership
Partner's interest in the Partnership	AHA tenancy is included on the Land Capital Account of the Partnership	As the tenancy is an asset of the partnership it is not valued separately but as part of the partner's interests in the business assets owned by the partnership

Partner who also owns the freehold land		
Partner lets the property to a tenant and farms in partnership with him/her.	Death of tenant who is also in partnership with the landlord. Landlord is not a tenant.	The tenancy has a negligible value as it is regarded as terminable. The sole surviving partner can as landowner serve a Section G notice on the Personal Representatives of the tenant. A succession of that tenancy by a family member is not relevant for the valuation as a potential succession is treated as a separate asset.
Partner who also has a leasehold interest in the land		
Partner lets the property to himself and another who farm in partnership together	Death of co-partner and co-tenant	This would be the same as above if the Partnership Agreement states that the tenancy is non-assignable. The partnership potentially could continue after the death of the co-tenant.
Partner lets the property to himself and another who farm in partnership together	Death of co-partner and tenant	A capitalised rent if the tenancy accrues to the surviving tenant but that person does not have any rights to inherit the partnership interest. In other words the right to be a tenant with the surviving joint tenant falls into the estate of the deceased partner and not to the surviving partner
Landowner with majority interest in partnership	If Partner dies as landowner and joint tenant	This follows the Gray case and the freehold reversion and the leasehold interests would be combined to give a greater value.

7.12 Debts of the partnership

Section 9 of the Partnership Act, 1890 states that "*every partner is liable jointly with the other partners ..... for all debts and obligations of the firm incurred while he is a partner; and after his death his estate is also severally liable in a due course of administration for such debts and obligations*". This means that the partnership debts and liabilities for which the deceased partner was jointly and severally liable, survive his death and are payable by his estate. It is therefore necessary for the administration of the estate to remain open until those debts can be ascertained. Potentially this could be as long as six years after the date of death (the expiry of the limitation period) unless the personal representatives rely on indemnities from the surviving partners. It is therefore wise for the personal representatives to seek clarification and, if appropriate, indemnities sooner rather than later. However, in accordance with section 36(3) of the Partnership Act, 1890, the estate is not liable for partnership debts contracted after the date of the death.

7.13 Partner's Wills

Whilst a Will may specify how the deceased partner would like his or her interest in the partnership to be disposed of, it does need to dovetail into what the partnership agreement says. The key point is that anyone taking instructions on the preparation of new Wills, where the testator is a partner in a farming business, should check not only the legal title to the property considered to be the farm but also the partnership agreement itself. If the farming partnership agreement specifies how the deceased partner's interest and share of the partnership is devolved, the terms of the partnership agreement would override the provisions of the Will. Take the example of Alex, Angus and Michael who form a partnership in 2010 and enter into a partnership agreement at the same time. The partnership agreement provides that on the death of a partner the deceased's partner's interest passes to the surviving partners in equal shares. Angus had married Sarah in 2015 and he decided to make a new Will which gave his share in the partnership to Sarah. Angus dies in 2019 and it is concluded (much to Sarah's dismay) that Angus' share was not his to give at the time of his death and that the provisions of the 2010 Partnership Agreement take precedence. Sarah's only option would be to make a claim against the Estate under the Inheritance (Provision for Family and Dependents) Act, 1975. Whilst the example does not preclude a claim for Business Property Relief being made, as Angus was unable to freely dispose of his partnership share, it may affect the valuation of his interest in the partnership for inheritance tax purposes.

On the basis that there are no contrary provisions in the partnership agreement, a partner can dispose of his interest and share in the partnership by a Will. It must be remembered that this share of the partnership is not a share in any specific property or asset but a *"share which the partner in question is entitled to recover at the conclusion of the winding up process"* (*Sandhu v Gill EWCA Civ 1297*). In other words, the capital, capital profits and current income accounts once all the debts and liabilities of the partnership have been realised and paid. In terms of Will drafting, it is therefore sensible for the Will to specify the partnership business not necessarily specific property held within the business.

In the case of *Moore (by his litigation friend, Moore) v Moore and another (2016) EWHC 2202 (Ch)* the property in question, Manor Farm, had been owned by the Moore family for four generations. Since the mid 1960s, the business had been run in a partnership initially between three brothers, Roger, Geoffrey and Richard. Since 2008, the partners were Roger, his son Stephen and a limited company called Till Valley Contracting Limited. In later years, Roger's mental health had deteriorated and as a consequence his active role in the partnership had declined to the extent that Stephen had in effect, run the farm on his own. The 2007 Will which had been drawn up failed to deal with the farming assets or Roger's share in the partnership which, under the Wills as prepared, would have fallen into the residuary estate and not follow the specific gift of the farm.

If Land has been introduced into the farm partnership and held on a capital account, a specific gift of that land in the Will is likely to be ineffective because the testator no longer holds an interest in land but an interest in the farming partnership. Julia and Fred form a partnership together in which Julia has a 52% and Fred a 48% interest in the land capital of Green Acre Farm. Fred subsequently goes to see another solicitor to make a Will and the Will is drawn up to give a specific gift of a 48% beneficial interest in Green Acre Farm to Victoria. A few years later Fred dies in a boating accident. The gift of the beneficial interest in the Farm to Victoria fails as at the moment of his death he did not have an interest in the farm merely a debt of the partnership capital. This is a good example of private client practitioners not checking the partnership agreement and the client perhaps not fully understanding the nature of their interests. The small glimmer of hope if you find a negligent Will where this has happened is where a partnership is solvent and there are other partnership assets that can bear the burden of the debts and liabilities of the partnership. In this circumstance the courts have upheld gifts of particular assets in the Will (*Re Holland (1907) 2 Ch 88*). The judge in this case upheld a gift of partnership assets to named beneficiaries in a Will as the testator could gift assets free of partnership debts as there were sufficient other assets in the partnership to meet any liability. However, it is far better to get it right first time and not rely on a hundred year-old case. *Re Holland* will also not help where the partnership is insolvent at the moment of death as demonstrated in the case of *Farquhar v Hadden (1871) LR7 Ch App 1*. In this case, the partnership property was subject to the payment of the partnership debts and so the testamentary gift of the partnership leasehold interests failed.

Unless the partnership agreement specifically mentions it, there is no right for the personal representatives to recover a specific property which had been held previously on the land capital account. The decision as to how the debt owed to the estate of the deceased partner is repaid is with the surviving partners. Often an agreement can be reached between the personal representatives and the continuing partners and in these cases the partners will appropriate real property rather than liquid assets. This may have the incentive for the continuing partners in assisting the business cash flow situation. However, there is no obligation for them to do so. If there is a desire for a specific property to be left to the deceased partner's wife or children, such as the farmhouse or an area of land with development potential, this needs to be specified in the partnership agreement.

The intentions of the family as expressed in the partner's respective Wills can be helpful evidence in clarifying matters particularly on cases as to whether land is intended to be held for the benefit of the partnership on land capital accounts or held outside of the business but used by the partnership. This question arose in the case of *Ham v Bell and others (2016) EWHC 1791 (Ch)* the same solicitor who had drafted the partnership agreement also had drafted the Wills of Mr and Mrs Ham. The Court took into account the provisions of the parent's Wills and noted that they disposed of their interests in the farmland in their Wills; bequests which would have been ineffective if the land had been a partnership asset.

7.14 Potential increase in the costs of Probate fees

A stir of anxiety arose from probate practitioners in early 2019 when there was an attempt by the Government to increase the probate court fees by up to 2,700 per cent resulting in a fee of up to £6,000 payable. These proposals were finally dropped with an assurance to look at them again as part of a wider review to make sure all fees are fair and reasonable. If partnership property is being held jointly by the partners then a grant of probate is not necessary to devolve the legal title to the property to the continuing partners. If future increases in probate fees are introduced then the use of jointly owned partnership property may be a way to mitigate the need to pay these higher fees.

7.15 Key decisions of the personal representatives

In summary, when a deceased partner dies there are a number of key decisions the personal representatives will need to take or be aware of:

- To elect, in accordance with section 42 of the Partnership Act, 1890, to receive a share of the profits made since the date of dissolution as are attributable to the deceased's share of the partnership or annual interest at 5% on the amount of the deceased's share of the partnership assets; and

- To decide to join the partnership as partners with the consent of the other partners;

- To serve notice for the partnership to dissolve;

- To establish whether any specific property is to be allocated to the deceased's partner's share. Unless the partnership agreement specifically mentions it, there is no right for the personal representatives to recover a specific property; only a right to acquire cash once all the debts and liabilities have been paid.

CHAPTER EIGHT
SUCCESSION PLANNING OF THE FAMILY FARM AND THE USE OF PARTNERSHIPS

Every partnership will be different and therefore will require specific clauses to take into account the client's needs, the circumstances and desires. Some of the bigger issues affecting farming partnerships are covered in other chapters. This chapter considers a smorgasbord of clauses and issues which should be considered by prospective partners and their professional advisors.

8.1 Parties to the agreement and recitals

Obvious it may be but worth mentioning that any partnership agreement should clearly identify the partners. Provision can be made at this stage to deal with who will be the senior or junior partners as well as whether the parties are full equity partners or partners with only limited rights to participate in profits and in the management of the business. The recitals are also a useful way to set out the history of the business and how it has evolved over time. An opportunity to tell a story about the conduct of the farm over a period of time. If for no other reason than to have something to refer HMRC to when you are claiming agricultural property relief or business property relief for inheritance tax purposes.

Finally use the recitals to either record or reinforce the status of any land being used by the partnership and whether individual partners hold that property on trust for the partnership or are allowing the partnership to occupy it under licence.

8.2 Commencement and duration of the partnership

There is no need for a partnership agreement to specify a commencement date, but it is useful to have one as it will provide certainty for when the partners will be liable for acts of co-partners and for the debts and obligations of the partnership. Where a written partnership agreement does not state a specific date then the inference would be that the partnership started on the date the agreement was completed. This would be the case unless other evidence can be brought in to prove that the partners had commenced the business at an earlier date.

As a criteria for the establishment of a partnership does not include the need to have a written partnership agreement, it could be that the partnership commenced prior to the agreement being completed. In which case, the partnership agreement should state the date the partnership actually commenced. This also works the other way around, where the agreement is completed before the commencement of the partnership as the agreement cannot regulate a non-existent relationship.

It is quite common for a farming partnership agreement to state that the partnership will continue until such time as it is terminated by the serving of the relevant notice by one of the partners in accordance with the terms of the agreement. Alternatively, the partnership could be for a fixed term of years or for the joint lives of the partners. In which case the agreement will need to specify this. In conjunction with considerations of the term of the partnership, provisions also need to be made as to when it can be terminated and whether this is by retirement, death or the serving of the appropriate notice.

8.3 Nature of the business

In other words, what does the partnership business actually do. The word farming needs to be included but also consider what other diversified elements are being undertaken by the business. If the partners decide at a future date to diversify the core farming business then restrictive wording in the partnership agreement does not preclude them from so doing but it will require the consent of all of the partners before it can be undertaken. When considering a claim for Agricultural Property Relief, the inclusion of the farming activities can be helpful to any claim.

8.4 Retirement

Quite rare for farmers to retire but it can happen. If there is no provision for retirement in the partnership agreement, section 33 of the Partnership Act, 1890 provides that the partnership will automatically be dissolved. An unplanned dissolution of the partnership should be avoided and so it is important that the partnership agreement makes provision for retirement. Similar considerations are needed to that of the death of a partner and much of this has already been covered in chapter 7 such as whether there is an option for the continuing partners to buy out the outgoing partner's share, the value to be placed on that share and whether any payments owed to the outgoing partner is paid as a lump sum or in instalments. It is also useful for the agreement to specify the notice that the partner wishing to retire has to give to his or her co-partners.

8.5 Banking

It is standard practice for the partnership agreement to name the bank in which is held the partnership bank account. Often for multi-generational farming partnerships there is a restriction on the account on what can be withdrawn at any one time without the consent of more than one partner or a senior and junior partner. This is designed to give comfort, particularly to the senior generation, that the junior and perhaps more enthusiastic partners are not going to spend all the capital cash on something which they would be uncomfortable with or feel that with their experience the money could be better spent elsewhere.

Most modern partnership agreements have express powers to draw cheques and this should be in accordance with the mandate at the bank. But what about internet banking and electronic transfers? It is therefore sensible to have specific provisions dealing with the authority on electronic banking as well.

8.6 Books and Accounts

It is usual for farming partnership agreements to contain provisions governing the maintenance of the partnership books and the preparation of the accounts. It is helpful for the relevant clauses to contain a provision that the partnership books are kept and maintained at the farmhouse. The point behind this provision is to re-enforce any claim for Agricultural Property Relief on the farmhouse that the partnership business is being run from the property. It is also a helpful reminder to the partners that the partnership business is actually run from the farmhouse.

8.7 Expulsion

Under the Partnership Act, 1890 there is no implied power to expel a partner. It therefore needs to be expressly included within the partnership agreement. It would be hoped that in a farming family partnership context it would never be needed but nevertheless the option ought to be there particularly for persistent breaches of the agreement, dishonesty or bankruptcy. The decision to expel a partner needs to be procedurally fair and that includes an opportunity for the accused partner to explain himself. It cannot be used for ulterior motives by another partner or simply because a partner disagrees with the strategic future of the business. If one gets to a point where the trusted relationship between the partners has irretrievably broken down then it might be wise to consider a general dissolution of the partnership.

The agreement will need to set out the procedures which should be followed including whether the decision to expel the partner has to be unanimous by the other partners or simply requires a majority vote. Like a retirement and the death of a partner, the agreement may want to have provisions concerning the purchase of the expelled partner's share of the business.

One particular nuance to consider for farming is whether the expelled partner is a freehold owner of the land upon which the business is being run. Would expelling that partner and the bad feeling that is likely to bring, be detrimental to the future farming business? If there is a fixed term lease in place with several years to run perhaps less of a problem than a licence arrangement which could be terminated at short notice. The message here is to think carefully and plan before actioning such a provision.

8.8 Assignment of a Partnership Share

Richard and Sarah had farming in partnership for many years. A few years later, Harriet was brought into the partnership and she has proved her worth as a junior partner. The parents have now decided to hand over part of their land capital account to Harriet. As she lives already on the farm in one of the cottages, the intention is for that part of the farm to pass over to her. Since she is already a partner then this is affected by a simple assignment of capital between one partner and the other, recorded by a partnership memorandum and an appropriate adjustment is made in the accounts.

Contrast this situation with an assignment of an interest to someone who is not an existing partner in the business. A mere assignment of a partner's interest to another does not necessarily make that person a partner. That requires the consent of the other partners unless there is a specific provision within the partnership agreement. Suppose Michael, Richard and Peter farmed in partnership together. They are brothers and farm quite happily together. Richard's wife, Stephanie, however, has a volatile relationship with Michael and Peter and whilst they tolerate her from afar they would not want to go into business with her. Richard decides to assign fifty per cent of his share in the partnership to Stephanie. Under no circumstances would Michael or Peter want Stephanie involved in the management of the business. In fact the less they have to do with her the better. The comfort for the brothers comes in section 31(1) of the Partnership Act, 1890 which says "*an assignment by any partner of his share in the partnership ..... does not ...... entitle the assignee .... to interfere in the management or administration of the partnership business or affairs*". Stephanie as the assignee has very restricted control of the partnership assets. She cannot interfere in the management of the business, or require any accounts of the transactions or sight of the partnership books.

Her rights (such as they are) is the right to the share of the profits to which Richard would otherwise be entitled to. In accordance with section 24(7) of the Partnership Act, 1890 new partners may only be admitted with the unanimous consent of the existing partners, unless the partnership agreement provides otherwise. Until that consent is given she has no rights to challenge the bona fide acts of management in the farming business. In *Re Garwood's Trusts (1903) 1 Ch 236* the assignee (Mrs Garwood) sought to have the payments of salaries to the partners stopped and it was held, applying section 31, that the decision to pay the salaries was a matter within the administration or management of the firm and so a decision of the partners to which she could not interfere. She had to accept the amount of profits as agreed between the partners.

There is some doubt as to whether an assignee acquires any liability for partnership losses. If he or she is being held out as a partner then they would be liable by virtue of section 14 of the Partnership Act, 1890 to third parties but otherwise section 31(1) seems to exempt him or her from being liable for losses.

8.9 Asset protection clauses

Pre-nuptial agreements are not enforceable in the English Courts, but recent case law has shown that judges are prepared to give them substantial weight and uphold them as long as certain precautionary steps were taken when the agreement was drawn up and signed. Nevertheless farming families have looked, in recent years, at other ways to protect the farm from a partner getting divorced. This has included provisions within the partnership agreement that any assignment of capital by a partner has to be to a blood relative of that partner or to a trust of which a blood relative is the beneficiary. These type of provisions within a farming partnership have yet to be fully scrutinised by the Family Courts and it therefore remains open as to the view they may take on these arrangements. Factors likely to be considered are the rationale behind having such a provision, what other assets are at the divorcing couple's disposal, the income position, length of marriage and the maintenance of any children.

CHAPTER NINE
CAPACITY ISSUES AND THE ELDERLY FARMER

Farming typically has an ageing workforce with now over a third of agricultural business owners being aged 65 or over. The average age of farmers in the UK increased from 51 to 60 in the three years from 2013 to 2016. Farming is a vocation; a way of life and it is not something which many in the industry aspire to retire from. The saying "a farmer dies with his boots on" is not without an element of truth. Nor does the current capital taxes legislation actively encourage retirement for the elderly farmer. In fact, with the potential loss of the valuable Agricultural Property Relief for Inheritance Tax purposes on the farmhouse for a retired farmer, actively works against the notion of retiring from farming.

Farming is also a hazardous industry with farmers working daily with potentially dangerous machinery, chemicals and livestock. The agricultural industry is one of the most high-risk industry sectors and accidents and injuries occur often. Accidents sadly often happen which potentially could leave a partner mentally or physically impaired.

These facts bring their own challenges to business owners in the agricultural sector as there is a chance that one or more partners may at some point suffer from mental or physical incapacity. How should the partnership business be structured to protect itself from the incapacity of a partner? Does the incapacity of a partner prevent the partnership from functioning and what steps should be taken if a partner suffers from mental or physical incapacity.

9.1 Family member joining into a partnership with fluctuating capacity

In general, there is nothing to prevent the creation or continuance of a farming partnership if a partner is incapacitated. Therefore it is quite possible for someone suffering a mental disorder as defined in the Mental Health Act, 1983 or mental incapacity under the Mental Capacity Act, 2005 to enter into partnership with another. This is with the proviso that the co-partners acted bona fide and were unaware of the incapacity. The stumbling block with this rule is that farming partnerships are mainly family affairs and like any close family it would be difficult to hide an illness of this nature. So whilst a third party may not be aware of an incapacity, it is reasonable to assume that a family member would be aware of the issue.

But what about the example of Bill? Bill had been farming as a sole trader for over sixty years and whilst his two sons, Ed and Scott, had worked on the farm as employees they were not themselves owners in the business. As Bill was approaching 80 the family (with the professional advice from the solicitors) had decided to restructure the business and bring Ed and Scott into partnership with Bill. This would relieve Bill of some of the management responsibility, ensure that the business would continue seamlessly after the death of Bill and enable succession planning to begin. The difficulty is that Ed and Scott have become increasingly aware that some days their father was becoming forgetful and absent minded. Following consultation with the doctors, Bill was diagnosed with the early stages of dementia. So in this case, Bill's capacity to enter into the partnership is questionable. What steps should now be taken to protect Bill and the business?

Clearly a Lasting Power of Attorney for Property and Financial Affairs should be recommended perhaps appointing Ed and Scott jointly and severally as the attorneys. This would assist in helping Bill to manage the farming business but does not help with the smooth continuity of the existing business on Bill's death. So, the desirability of a partnership for the future of the business remains attractive.

9. CAPACITY ISSUES AND THE ELDERLY FARMER • 99

As an ordinary farming partnership does not have its own legal personality, each individual partner is assessed on his or her own capacity to enter into the partnership. Whilst the law governing capacity is governed by common law there is an interaction with the Mental Capacity Act, 2005 as this allows the Courts to approach questions of capacity through the tests established by the common law. Bill is presumed to have capacity to enter into the partnership and the tests to ensure that he did have capacity is time and place specific. In the case of *Fehily v Atkinson (2016) EWHC 3069 (Ch)* the Court identified five principles to assess a person's capacity to enter into a contract. It would therefore be possible for Bill to enter into the partnership on the basis that at the time of signing he could satisfy the following:

1. A recognition of the issues that must be considered when entering into a partnership, including an understanding of the reasons and implications of entering into the partnership and an understanding of the effect of the main clauses of the partnership agreement;

2. Sufficient capacity to make the decision to enter into the partnership with Ed and Scott even if the complexities of the taxation of partnerships may be beyond him. It is the capacity for the specific issue which is being judged (i.e entering into the partnership) even if he does not have capacity to make other decisions on the future running of the farm;

3. Sufficient capacity at the time of signing the partnership agreement. This would be the case even if 10 minutes later, Bill has forgotten that he has signed the agreement;

4. An ability to understand the nature of entering into partnership. This is not whether Bill actually understood the partnership but instead whether he had the ability to understand if the consequences had been fully explained to him; and

5. Assistance with understanding the partnership agreement from the lawyer or accountant does not prevent Bill from having capacity to understand it. Afterall a partnership agreement is

often a long legal document and can be confusing to read if you are not used to such legal documents. If a professional advisor has been instructed to assist the family then it is important to establish whether they did have the insight and understanding to realise that advice was needed, the ability to find and instruct an appropriate professional advisor and the capacity to understand and make decisions based on that advice.

Particularly in view of the fifth principle, if faced with this situation then it would be advisable that the partner who may be suffering from fluctuating capacity to be separately represented from his or her co-partners. That way, you can be assured that any future queries on undue influence and conflicts of interest have been dealt with. It would also be sensible for a full capacity assessment report to be commissioned from a suitably experience medical practitioner.

9.2 Existing partner in a farming partnership loses capacity

Probably more common is the situation where an existing partner in the business loses capacity. So instead of Bill being a sole trader for the last fifty years at some point he joined Ed and Scott and ran the business through a partnership. A person's incapacity will not, on its own, dissolve the partnership. The person suffering will still be entitled to the profits arising from his share of the partnership and he will also still be responsible for his portion of the debts and liabilities of the partnership.

In old farming partnership agreements, you may come across a clause which states that on the mental incapacity of a partner, that partner is deemed to have retired from the partnership with immediate effect. In other words, the incapacitated partner is kicked out of the partnership. Such clauses are now deemed voidable. This is because under the Equality Act, 2010 such clauses would be regarded as discrimination.

If there is a registered Enduring Power of Attorney or Lasting Power of Attorney – Property & Financial Affairs then the attorneys will be able to step into the incapacitated partner's shoes in order for the business to continue to be administered with certain restrictions without first applying for a Court Order (see below).

The Court of Protection has authority and power under section 18(1)(d) to carry on, on the partner's behalf, "*any profession, trade or business*". So it is perfectly possible for the farming partnership business to continue if one of the partner's loses capacity and indeed, with Agricultural Property Relief and Business Property Relief for inheritance tax purposes it may even be desirable to keep the person in the partnership.

9.3 Powers of Attorney

It is sensible for everyone, not just farmers to have as a minimum a Lasting Power of Attorney – Property & Financial Affairs in place. If someone loses capacity and they do not have a valid enduring or lasting power of attorney in place then there would be a need to apply to the Court of Protection to seek the appointment of a Deputy to run the business. We have already seen that the Court has the power under section 18(1)(d) of the Mental Capacity Act, 2005 to give an order to allow the Deputy to run the business but these things take time. In the interim no decisions which require the authority of the incapacitated partner could take place and this could be detrimental to the future of the business.

A partner may wish (and indeed it may be preferable) to have different attorneys to deal with his personal financial matters and those business matters relating to the partnership. In which case, it is sensible to have two Lasting Powers of Attorney. One to deal with the donor's personal affairs and a second Business Lasting Power of Attorney. Denzil Lush has commented that there are "cases where the donor should have made the LPAs: one for their business affairs and the other for their personal affairs" (Lush (2013) Eld LJ 144). A Business Lasting Power of Attorney allows the donor (the partner) to appoint an attorney to make decisions concerning their business interests either when they are unavailable or when they lack mental capacity. It is an extension of the management of the business and is aimed at reducing risk to the business. Examples of the types of decisions the attorneys can make under a Business Lasting Power of Attorney include signing contracts, the sale or acquisition of partnership property, paying wages and hiring or removing employees of the partnership.

When taking instructions for a Business Lasting Power of Attorney as well as the usual instructions and assessment for a usual Lasting Power of Attorney, you also need to understand how the farming business operates and the management and decision-making structure. In this regard sight of the current partnership agreement is essential. This will also assist when drafting the appropriate memorandum of wishes detailing how the donor would wish his business interests in the farm to run if he still had capacity, his values and beliefs and the weighting of those in making any decisions. As the memorandum of wishes is for information purposes only and cannot compel an attorney to make decisions in a particular way, then any reference to the memorandum of wishes in the Business Lasting Power of Attorney is likely to be severed by the Court of Protection.

Bill has two sons who are already involved in the farming business (Ed and Scott). They already have knowledge on how the farming partnership works whereas Bill's daughter, Harriet and his wife, Alison have never been involved in the farming business. Bill therefore could have Ed and Scott appointed as his business attorneys and Harriet and Alison as his attorneys to deal with his personal financial matters. Both Lasting Powers of Attorney will act concurrently with each other and each will make it clear where their authority starts and ends.

It is clearly important that the right attorneys are chosen. It not only needs to be someone the donor can trust but also someone who has an understanding of farming and the challenges that running an agricultural business brings. Practice 7.8 of the Mental Capacity Act Code emphasises the importance of choosing the attorney carefully. The person chosen should be trustworthy, competent and reliable but above all they must have the appropriate skills and ability to carry out the necessary tasks. The donor would be well advised to think again if the attorneys chosen have no experience or knowledge of running a farming business.

The attorney should appreciate, in relation to the farming business any contractual obligations, health and safety issues, insurance, risks, compliance paperwork, subsidies, tax and employment issues. That does not mean they have to have expert knowledge but they need to realise when they should ask for further advice before making a specific decision. If the attorney does not possess the appropriate skills and a full understanding of the donor's role and responsibilities within the partnership then they may be liable to the business. In the Scottish case of *Ross Harper & Murphy v Scott Banks (2000) SCLR 736*, the Court held that "*a partner may in certain circumstances be liable in damages to his firm …. a standard which requires the exercise of reasonable care in all the relevant circumstances*".

When choosing the attorneys it is also important that the donor considers how the delegation of a partner's authority will impact on the other partners. It is a recipe for a disaster to have someone appointed as attorney who does not get along with the other partners. In the case of *Moore (by his litigation friend, Moore) v Moore and another (2016) EWHC 2202 (Ch)* the property in question, Manor Farm, was owned by the Moore family. Since 2008, the partners were Roger, his son Stephen and a limited company called Till Valley Contracting Limited. In later years Roger's mental health had deteriorated and as a consequence his active role in the partnership had declined to the extent that Stephen had in effect run the farm on his own. Roger had appointed his wife (and Stephen's mother) to be an attorney under a Lasting Power of Attorney. However, there was a volatile relationship between mother and son particularly because she felt that Stephen's siblings also ought to benefit from the farm after Roger's death. In hindsight was Roger's wife the best person to be appointed as an attorney in relation to the farming business?

You may also need to consider conflicts of interest between the donor and the attorney as well as the attorney of a Lasting Power of Attorney relating specifically to the donor's personal affairs and those of the business. A perceived conflict may arise, for example, where the voting rights of the Donor Partner is 40% and the attorney (also a partner) has 20% voting rights. The attorney attends a partnership meeting and even though the other partners know the attorney makes decisions using the donor's 40% and his or her own 20% separately, a perceived conflict might arise, at the attorney may seemingly have a controlling 60% vote.

9.4 Delegation authority

The Partnership Act, 1890 is silent on delegation. This means that the authority to delegate roles and functions to other partners needs to stem from the partnership agreement itself. This will include authority to delegate under a General Power of Attorney, an Enduring Power of Attorney or a Lasting Power of Attorney.

Further delegation by someone who has already been delegated to can only occur with the specific authority from the partnership agreement.

As we have seen Limited Liability Partnerships are subject to many of the provisions of the Companies Act, 2006. It is, therefore, important that you check the provisions of the Limited Liability Partnership Agreement to see if there are any restrictions on the delegation of authority to a third party.

9.5 Position if a person has lost capacity – entering into a partnership

Suppose Bill had lost capacity to enter into a partnership but had signed a Lasting Power of Attorney. Could the attorneys (Ed and Scott) enter into a partnership arrangement on Bill's behalf? This is a grey area but the answer is probably not. As one of the guiding principles under the Mental Capacity Act, 2005, the attorneys have to act in the donor's best interests. It might be in the best interests of Ed and Scott for Bill to enter into a partnership relationship as it improves the inheritance tax position on Bill's death as well as assist with the continuity of the business, but is it really in Bill's best interests? Certainly the Court of Protection will be resistant to anything which benefits the children but does not materially benefit Bill. Even if it could be argued that there was a benefit to Bill, would such a benefit outweigh the risks of entering into an arrangement where Bill will be liable for the debts and liabilities of the partnership?

There is then the question of conflicts of interest and acting in the Donor's best interests, particularly, as in the case above, the co-partners would also be the attorneys. Decisions which may be in the best interests of the partnership may not be in Bill's personal best interests. A partner's duty of care is to act in the best interests of the partnership but that may be contrary to Bill's best interests.

Whilst the Lasting Power of Attorney may give the attorney's authority to made decisions on the Donor's property and financial affairs, it is hard to see that making decisions about the Donor's interests in an existing partnership (if there is one) could be stretched to include decisions as to whether or not to enter into a partnership in the first place. Though the Court of Protection has powers to make decisions, or appoint a Deputy to make decisions under section 18(1)(d) of the Mental Capacity Act, 2005 to carry on the business, does this really extend to changing an existing sole trade business into a partnership or starting a new partnership?

As we have seen, as a general point it is possible to delegate functions to an attorney, but it is important to consider the nature of the partnership and whether it should be inferred that personal performance is one of the partnership's obligations as a power of attorney cannot delegate actions of a personal nature. If an attorney is acting under the terms of a delegated function then this needs to be made clear to third parties otherwise there is a danger of the attorney being caught by the provisions of section 14 of the Partnership Act, 1890 as being held out as a partner and so personally liable for the partnership's liabilities.

Perhaps as an alternative to Scott and Ed entering into partnership with Bill, they could consider granting a Farm Business Tenancy to a new partnership of which the partners would be themselves. Whilst a Court Order is probably necessary and the terms would need to be negotiated at arm's length, this negates any doubt as to their authority to enter into partnership and does also assist in mitigating some of the potential inheritance liability on Bill's death.

9.6 The importance of the protection of APR and BPR if a partner loses capacity

Even though a dwelling might in other respects qualify as a farmhouse, it will not qualify for Agricultural Property Relief unless it is occupied for the purposes of agriculture. Given the current HMRC view that the farmhouse must be the centre of farming operations, there must be a difficulty where, on the facts, the farmer is no longer well enough to look after the land. In *Executors of Atkinson Deceased v HMRC (2011) UTUK FTC/61/2010*, Mr Atkinson's health had deteriorated to the point that he was, at the time of his death, living in a care home. Mr Atkinson had been in partnership with his son and daughter-in-law from 1980. He granted a tenancy of the farm to the partnership and this was treated as an asset of the partnership. The property subject to the lease included a bungalow which had been occupied by Mr Atkinson and remained furnished even when he moved into a care home. The question before the Upper Tribunal was whether the bungalow was a farmhouse for the purposes of the relief. The Tribunal held that the occupation was not by Mr Atkinson as the farmer but by the partnership and that partnership had ceased to occupy the bungalow when Mr Atkinson moved into the care home. It was necessary to identify a strong connection between the use of the bungalow and the agricultural activities being carried out on the farm. The mere housing of personal belongings and the occasional attendance at the property was not sufficient for these purposes.

If, instead the partner lacking capacity occupied the farmhouse and if the attorneys appointed under the Lasting Power of Attorney continue to occupy, or take up occupation of, the farmhouse in order to care for the partner, this should assist in any Agricultural Property Relief claim on the farmhouse.

From a Business Property Relief point of view, if the attorneys appointed under a Lasting Power of Attorney are all involved in the management of the partnership business, this should help to ensure that the partner lacking capacity is effectively still trading at the time of his or her death and will therefore assist in the claim for Business Property Relief on the partnership assets attributed to that person.

9.7 Ability to dissolve a partnership

Section 35 gives a number of grounds on which a Court can order the dissolution of a partnership. On application by a partner, the Court may decree a dissolution under section 35(b) *"when a partner ..... becomes in any other way permanently incapable of performing his part of the partnership contract"* but this can only apply where the partner is permanently incapable. It therefore will not apply to a diminution of capacity or a temporary illness or incapacity. In this case, it would be appropriate for the other partner or partners to apply to the Court under section 35(f) which gives the Court power where *"in the opinion of the Court, render it just and equitable that the partnership be dissolved"*.

If there is a registered Enduring Power of Attorney, a Lasting Power of Attorney or a Deputy has been appointed then the Court of Protection can give the Attorney or Deputy authority under section 18(1) of the Mental Capacity Act, 2005 to service a notice of retirement or dissolution under the partnership agreement as well as the initiation of proceedings under section 35 of the Partnership Act, 1890. The problem is that the power under section 18(1) can only be used when there are no disputes in relation to the partnership accounts or partnership agreement. The Court of Protection has no jurisdiction to deal with partnership disputes. In the absence of an Attorney or Deputy, however, there is doubt whether the Court of Protection has the power itself to order a dissolution.

9.8 Authority to transfer partnership capital

Suppose Bill has been in partnership with Ed and Scott for a number of years and the partnership assets include Manor Farm. This is credited entirely to Bill's land capital account. A few of the fields on the edge of the nearby village have been ring-fenced for development and to maximise the availability of Business Asset Disposal Relief for capital gains tax purposes it has been advised by the accountant to transfer part of these fields to Ed and Scott. Bill has sufficient resources and income from his other assets and so has no need to receive entirely the proceeds of sale from the development site. As Ed and Scott are Bill's attorneys under a Lasting Power of Attorney they consider an application to the Court of Protection for an Order to make the gift of land capital from Bill to themselves.

As far as any gift element is concerned, most proposed gifts are not given on a customary occasion and therefore do now fall within section 12 of the Mental Capacity Act, 2005. It therefore needs to be authorised by the Court of Protection under section 23(4). The Court should have regard to the affordability of the gift and the risk of the Donor being deprived of their means of support. This includes taking into account anticipated future needs. In other words, as in the case of Bill, the gift is being made from surplus funds.

In accordance with section 4 of the Mental Capacity Act, 2005, consideration then needs to be made of all the circumstances it would be reasonable to regard as relevant.

Firstly, wherever possible and as reasonably practical enable the Donor's participation in the decision.

Secondly, consider the Donor's past and present wishes and feelings. Is there any evidence that the Donor intended to make the gift, for example, past conduct? Is this the first time that he has given land capital to Ed and Scott or what does his Will say about the disposal of his assets after death?

Thirdly, consider the beliefs and values that would be likely to influence his decision if he had capacity. This could include a desire to pass on the Farm to the next generation or a belief that he would do all that is possible to mitigate any tax liability.

Fourthly, consider any other factors that he would be likely to consider if he were able to do so. This could include the costs of repairs or maintenance if the object of the gift was a redundant agricultural barn or equalisation the estate between different siblings or (as in the example above) the taxation consequences of making the gift i.e is holdover relief for capital gains tax purposes available?

Finally, you need to consider the views of anyone engaged in the caring of the Donor or interested in his welfare. The best way forward is to know that everyone agrees to the proposals but that is not always practically possible. At least three people should be notified and would include any co-attorneys and anyone who benefits under his Will.

9.9 Conflicts of interest

As have already been referred to, you should be very wary of conflicts of interest, particularly where the incapacitated person's attorneys are also his co-partners. Conflicts of interest inevitably arise in the Court of Protection jurisdiction and it is perfectly possible for the Donor to appoint someone to act where a conflict potentially exists (such as Bill appointing Ed and Scott) as long as the Donor does so in the knowledge of that conflict. When it does happen, the Court of Protection must reach a conclusion as to whether it is a conflict which can be sanctioned. There may very well be situations where a conflict is more apparent than real, and, in most cases, the apparent conflict should not automatically mean that the person is disqualified from acting. The problem may, in some cases be alleviated if an independent non-conflicted attorney is appointed as well.

CHAPTER TEN
DISSOLUTION OF THE BUSINESS

Sometimes, a partnership ends its natural life and comes to an end. Dissolution marks the legal end of a partnership at which point the assets will be sold, the debts and liabilities paid and the balance distributed to the partners. There are in fact, two distinct situations, each of which is termed a dissolution. The first, and the one we are looking at in detail in this chapter, is where the whole business is finished as a going concern and has to be wound up. In this case each of the former partners receive a share of the assets after the creditors have been paid. The second (often termed a technical dissolution) is where there is a retirement or death of a particular partner. The main issue here is the valuation of the outgoing partner's interest and this has been looked at in detail in chapter 8. The distinction between the two types of dissolution is important because the treatment of the assets of the partnership and the rights of the individual partners are different in each case. The question that needs to be asked each time will be is there a winding up or simply a buy out of the outgoing partner's share?

In terms of the Partnership Act, 1890 the relevant provisions which deal with dissolution are contained in sections 32 to 44. This can be sub divided to sections 32 to 35 which deal with the circumstances in which a partnership business can be wound up and sections 39 to 44 which deal with the financial rights between partners on dissolution or retirement.

10.1 Reasons for dissolution

There are many reasons why partnerships dissolve and amongst others can include the death or retirement of a partner, a general agreement to throw the towel in, a change in the business and farming dynamics making the need of a partnership obsolete as well as the hostile breakdown of family relationships. The latter example is demonstrated in the recent case of *Guest v Guest and Guest (2019) EWHC 869 (Ch)*. Here a partnership had been created in 2012 between David and Josephine Guest and their son Andrew to run the farming business at Trump Farm and the relationship had broken down because Andrew and his parents were at odds over whether the dairy herd should be expanded. This mistrust reached such heights that the parents started to record their conversations with their son. In April 2015, Andrew's parents served a notice on their son to dissolve the partnership, giving him and his family three months to leave their cottage at Trump Farm. Andrew in turn brought a proprietary estoppel claim against his parents on the basis that his parent's had made numerous representations over a long period that he would inherit a substantial part of Trump Farm and as a result Andrew had spent most of his working life working on the farm for low wages. The Court held that it would be unconscionable to allow his parents to go back on their promises and consequently awarded Andrew 50% of the partnership business and 40% of the underlying value of the farm.

10.2 Serving notice

Most farming partnerships continue for an unspecified duration. In other words when it is created it was not for a fixed period of time or purpose. These types of partnership are known as partnerships at will and continue until a partner serves notice for the partnership to dissolve in accordance with sections 26(1) or 32(c) of the Partnership Act, 1890. The other type of partnership is a partnership for a fixed term. These can only be ended in accordance with the terms of the partnership agreement, by operation of the Partnership Act (for example the death or bankruptcy of a partner under section 33) or by a court order. The presumption will be that a partnership is a partnership at will unless there is an express or implied agreement to the contrary.

For written partnership agreements it is advisable for there to be to a method of ending the partnership including a notice period to avoid a situation of an immediate dissolution. The reason for this is that a partnership at will can be ended at any time by one partner serving notice on his or her co-partners.

The right to dissolve a partnership at will is contained in section 26(1) of the Partnership Act, 1890 which states that "where no fixed term has been agreed upon for the duration of the partnership, *any partner may determine the partnership at any time on giving notice of his intentions so to do to all the other partners*". It is, however, important to read this provision in the context of section 32(1)(c) of the same Act. This provides that subject to contrary intention a partnership that is entered into for an undefined time is dissolved by any partner giving notice to his or her co-partners of the intention to dissolve the partnership. The practical difference between whether you serve a notice under section 26 or section 32(1)(c) is to consider whether the partnership agreement has any provisions within it as to termination, however vague. If it does then then section 26 cannot apply as there is a limitation to the duration of the partnership. Section 32(1)(c) can only apply subject to any contrary intention within the partnership agreement itself. Potentially the right to dissolve by notice can be excluded either by express or implied agreement.

On the basis that you are able to serve a notice to dissolve the partnership then it is not necessary for that notice to be in writing though clearly to avoid ambiguity as to when notice is served and when the partnership is dissolved, it is a good idea to do so. Any such notice can be given at any time and there is no need for there to be a reasonable period of notice. In the case of farming partnerships it may be advantageous for accounting purposes to serve notices to dissolve a partnership at an appropriate accounting date such as the end of the farming year, accounting year or tax year.

Any notice to dissolve must be clear and unambiguous and specify the date that the dissolution is to take effect from. It will, however, only be effective once it has been communicated to all the other partners.

10.3 Express clauses and mutual agreement

Modern farming partnership agreements are likely to include specific express dissolution clauses which expand the available grounds for dissolution specified in the Partnership Act, 1890. This is different to the power of expulsion of a particular partner and include when the relationships between the partners have completely broken down, when it is not possible for the continuing partners to buy out the interest of a partner who has died or retired and where a partner has withdrawn the land he has introduced into the partnership making it impossible for the farming business to continue.

It is also possible for partnerships to be ended by an express agreement of all the partners. Take the example of brothers Richard and Fred who have farmed two farms in partnership for twenty-five years. The natural life of the partnership has come to the end and for succession purposes each brother wants to pass an individual farm to their respective children. As part of the partition of the two farms the brothers agree that on 29 September the partnership is dissolved and this is minuted accordingly.

10.4 Court Order

Section 35 of the Partnership Act, 1890 contains five grounds on which a Court may order a dissolution of a partnership following an application to do so by a partner. When exercising its discretion, the court will consider other remedies available for resolving the particular issues including retirement or deemed retirement and expulsion of a partner.

Mental incapacity

We have already seen in Chapter 9 that that Court of Protection can, on behalf of the incapacitated partner, serve notice to dissolve the partnership under the Mental Capacity Act, 2005. The Court of Protection would, however, be unwilling to exercise this power where there are disputes under the partnership agreement or the partnership accounts. In which case, the alternative is for the partners to apply under section 35(b) of the Partnership Act, 1890 for an Order.

Permanent incapacity

Section 35(b) of the Partnership Act, 1890 refers to a partner becoming "*in any other way permanently incapable of performing his part of the partnership contract*". This relates not just to mental incapacity but also physically incapacity. However, the incapacity must be permanent. Manor Farm had been farmed in partnership by Jack, Richard and Tom for a number of years. Jack suffers from a stroke and Richard and Tom wish to dissolve the partnership. As the medical evidence of Jack's condition shows that his health is improving and that the probability of incapacity is only temporary in nature, it would not be possible for an Order to dissolve the partnership to be granted. It is for this reason that most farming partnership agreements (and prudent in view of the average age of farmers) will contain a clause to allow a dissolution if there is a minimum period of incapacity, say three months.

Conduct injurious to the partnership business

This requires proof that the conduct of the partner is "*calculated to prejudicially affect the carrying on of the business*". There is, however, no need to prove actual loss or public knowledge. An example would be a violent criminal act or an act which is dishonest in nature. Such an act might, for example, prevent a bank from lending money to that partnership and even though the act itself is not directly connected to farming the carrying out of that act has affected the viability of the business being carried on by the other partners.

Persistent breaches of the agreement

There are in fact two separate limbs. The first is a wilful or persistent breach of the partnership agreement and the second is conduct which makes the continuation of the business impracticable. The Court is reluctant to interfere in trivial partnership disputes and little sympathy will be given to over exaggerating the consequences of minor differences. Examples might include failure to account for sums received or failure to attend partnership meetings which has the effect of making the running of the farming business impossible.

Carrying on the business at a loss

At this time of change in the agricultural industry, the current economic climate and the changes to the way the Government subsidise farmers it may seem that this heading could, sadly, be used frequently in a farming context. As explained elsewhere, the whole point of running a business in a partnership is with a view to make a profit and the expectation that a profit can or will be made goes to the heart of the partnership relationship. Only where there is no prospect of a profit being made and the business can only be carried on at a loss will the Court dissolve a partnership. In the case of *Jennings v Baddeley (1856) 3 K & J, 78*, the partnership capital had been exhausted and some of the partners were unable or unwilling to contribute further funds.

Just and equitable ground

The final heading contained in section 35(f) of the Partnership Act, 1890, allows an order to be made *"whenever in any case circumstances have arisen which, in the opinion of the court, render it just and equitable that the partnership be dissolved"*. A typical example would be one where the mutual trust between the partners has broken down.

10.5 Winding up of the partnership business

Once a partnership has dissolved, the next step is to wind up the partnership business. For these purposes the partners retain authority to bind each other as far as is needed to wind up the partnership's affairs and complete any unfinished transactions but not to do anything further. If it is decided that the partners are going to conduct the winding up of the farming business themselves then they continue to do so as agents for their fellow partners. The authority for the partners to continue the business after dissolution for the purposes of winding up stems from section 38 of the Partnership Act, 1890 and includes acts such as receiving debts due, completing contracts, drawing cheques, securing the subsidy payment owed, fulfilling obligations under the stewardship schemes and harvesting and selling the growing crops. The authority does not extend to new business and contracts entered into after dissolution. Lord Reed in *Duncan v The MFV Marigold PD145 2006 SLT 975* commented that the authority to wind up "*cannot warrant the continuation of the business for more than a temporary period*".

10.6 Application of assets on a winding up

In accordance with section 39 of the Partnership Act, 1890 a partner is entitled to have the partnership property applied in payment of all the partnership's debts and liabilities. Any surplus is then divided between the partners in accordance with their entitlements. Subject to any contrary agreement the order of settlement of accounts between the partners is contained in section 44 of the Partnership Act, 1890 and the assets of the partnership are applied as follows:

- Losses (both of an income or capital nature) are paid out of profits, then capital and, if this is insufficient, by the partners individually in the proportions in which they are entitled to share profits (unless the partnership agreement states otherwise);

- Assets of the partnership are applied:
    - In paying the partnership's debts and liabilities of third parties;
    - In repaying any loans made by the partners to the partnership;
    - In paying each partner what that partner is entitled to in respect of capital (both general capital and land capital); and
    - Any residue is divided between the partners in the proportions in which profits are divided.

If there is sufficient assets to pay all the debts and liabilities of the partnership but not enough to repay all of the partners' capital, the amount of capital which cannot be repaid is treated as a loss and is divided between the partners in the proportions in which they are entitled to share in the capital profits. As we have already seen when considering section 24 of the Partnership Act, 1890, this could be equally unless otherwise agreed. Michael and Sarah (brother and sister) have both lent £25,000 to the partnership. In addition Michael has contributed £75,000 of capital whereas Sarah has only contributed £50,000 and it was agreed that any profits of a capital nature would be divided equally between them. On the winding up of the partnership, after the payment of all the debts and liabilities of the partnership, there is a surplus for distribution of £125,000. The monies lent by Sarah and Michael are repaid first (£25,000 each). This leaves a surplus of £75,000 which is less then the amount of capital originally contributed. The shortfall (£50,000) is treated as a loss which is divided equally between Michael and Sarah. Therefore Sarah receives £25,000 and Michael the remaining £50,000.

10.7 Buy out or Syers v Syers orders

The usual way of operating section 39 of the Partnership Act, 1890 in a winding up is to realise the partnership assets by a sale on the open market. In a farming context that is not always desirable particularly where there are members of the family who are willing to take on the farming business. In *Kingsley and others v Kingsley and another (2019) EWHC 1073 (Ch)*, the Court needed to consider whether a surviving partner of a farming partnership has the right to buy the farmland before it was sold on the open market. As the farmland was not a partnership asset but held by Roger and Sally as beneficial tenants in common then applying the provisions of sections 14 and 15 of the Trusts of Land and Appointment of Trustees Act, 1996 the farm would normally be sold. As there was a disagreement as to value between Sally and Roger's executors then the only way to definitively establish what something is worth is to sell it on the open market. Under the Trusts of Land and Appointment of Trustees Act, 1996, the Court has discretion to make orders whereby a party has the opportunity to purchase the interest and only failing this would the whole property be sold on the open market. Such reasoning was followed in the case of *Collins v Collins (No 2) (2015) EWHC 2652 (Ch)* which concerned the sale of farmland following the dissolution of a family partnership and where any members of the family were able to bid for it. There is nothing within the Partnership Act, 1890 which requires the assets of the partnership to be sold on the winding up of the partnership. The court can take the view that it is more preferable to require one or more of the partners to buy out the partner petitioning for dissolution and such orders are known as *Syers v Syers* orders after the House of Lords decision in that case *(1876) 1 App Cas 174*. In that case the Court ordered the majority partners to buy out the minority on the dissolution of the partnership. A Syers v Syers order is only available on a dissolution of a partnership and can relate to the entire minority's share or just specific assets.

10.8 Arbitration and Mediation

Rising land values, falling incomes and the inability of the farm to support more than one family are in part due to the increase in disputes arising out of farming partnerships. Sometimes this will lead to a full dissolution and winding up of the partnership which is often not what the family would have wanted. It is for this reason that often in partnership agreements there are arbitration and mediation provisions.

Most partnership agreements contain an arbitration clause which is binding on the partners. However this can be an expensive, time consuming and frustrating process and a resolution through the court process might seem an attractive alternative.

An increasingly effective alternative and cheaper than arbitration or court proceedings is mediation. If deployed at an early stage it can often help to defuse a dispute within the family but the partners cannot be forced to mediate and it therefore requires a willingness on both sides of a dispute to engage in the mediation process.

10.9 Proprietary Estoppel Claims

The agricultural world and farming partnerships in particular seem to be susceptible to proprietary estoppel claims. There have been a number of these cases in recent years, usually involving the child who has worked for a number of years on the farm being dissatisfied that he or she would not be receiving the farm.

In order to claim proprietary estoppel there must be an assurance of sufficient clarity, reliance by the person claiming on that assurance and evidence that the claimant has acted to his or her detriment as a result of that reliance. The general principle when considering the question of detriment is that counter-veiling benefits must be taken into account. In the case of *Moore v Moore (2016) EWHC 2202 (Ch)*, the son had been made a salaried partner in 1997 and an equity partner in 2008. The Court accepted the submissions that this was a legitimate device to mitigate the tax liability and the allocation of any profits did not generate so as to infer on him the de facto right to regard these monies as his own as of right to do as he wished. Therefore the admission of the son as a partner was not a counter-veiling benefit but rather was the start of the fulfilment of promises. It did not operate to reduce or extinguish the detriment suffered which was that the son had positioned his whole life around the farm in the expectation that he would inherit his father's share of it after both parents had passed away.

In the case of *Wild v Wild (2018) EWHC 2197 (Ch)*, two brothers had operated the dairy farm in partnership with their father and stepmother. As part of the proprietary estoppel claim, the Court was required to determine whether the farmhouse and bungalow were assets of the farming partnership and the case required a full analysis of what was and what was not partnership property. This included whether the properties were included in the balance sheet of the partnership accounts, the absence of rent and the use of funds to pay for improvements. In this case the Court concluded that neither properties were partnership property.

A similar analysis was carried out in *Guest v Guest and Guest (2019) EWHC 869 (Ch)* where David and Josephine Guest and their son

Andrew ran the partnership business. Andrew brought a proprietary estoppel claim against his parents on the basis that his parent's had made numerous representations over a long period that he would inherit a substantial part of Trump Farm and as a result Andrew had spent most of his working life working on the farm for low wages. The Court held that it would be unconscionable to allow his parents to go back on their promises and consequently awarded Andrew 50% of the partnership business and 40% of the underlying value of the farm.

In *Habberfield v Habberfield (2019) EWCA Civ 890* the Court of Appeal upheld the daughter's claim for proprietary estoppel following her detrimental reliance on her parents' assurances that she would inherit the farm. This was the case even though she had previously declined an offer to run the farm in partnership with her parents. The reason for the rejections of the proposal by her parents was that as one of three partners she would not have been in control as well as the proposal not offering her husband an immediate admission to the partnership. However this rejection was not enough to negate the detriment she had suffered for the thirty years of work on the farm based on the assurance that she would inherit it.

CHAPTER ELEVEN
STAMP DUTY LAND TAX

Under section 42 of the Finance Act, 2003, Stamp Duty Land Tax is payable on all transactions involving land and buildings situated in the UK. Any farming partnership where land is being brought onto the balance sheet, moving capital accounts between partners and dissolution of a partnership involving land, will need to consider the Stamp Duty Land Tax implications. Equally it is important to remember that if there is no land involved then no Stamp Duty Land Tax can be chargeable. Property held outside the partnership but used by the partnership is not included in any calculation of Stamp Duty Land Tax. The same considerations as to whether an interest is included or not is the same as to whether or not the land is partnership property as explored in Chapter 3. Just because the farming business is conducted on the Farm does not necessarily mean there would be a land transaction if the capital in the business was varied. This is another good reason why it is so important that the farm partnership agreement clearly identifies what land is included on the balance sheet and what land is held outside of the business but used by it.

For Stamp Duty Land Tax to apply there has to be a land transaction and this is defined as any acquisition of a chargeable interest which includes *"an estate, interest, right or power in or over land"* (section 48(1) Finance Act, 2003). This applies to all types of partnership whether it is an ordinary partnership, a limited partnership or a limited liability partnership. In this context a partnership is effectively transparent and the assets of the partnership are treated as being held by or on behalf of the partners.

The measure of a partner's interest in a partnership is calculated by reference to income and not capital sharing ratios and it is the movement of that interest which forms the basis as to how Stamp Duty Land Tax is calculated. The only time when the capital sharing ratios are relevant is where the movement could be constituted as the giving of consideration.

11.1 Transfer of a chargeable interest to a partnership

Ben and John are brothers and they have just taken on the family farm. They decide to go into partnership together and, on the advice of their accountants, they also bring the land onto the balance sheet of the partnership. The land was previously owned by them equally. How is bringing the land onto the balance sheet of a partnership treated for Stamp Duty Land Tax purposes? As has already been mentioned the bringing of land into the partnership is an event where Stamp Duty Land Tax needs to be considered as it is a relevant land transaction. Paragraph 10 of Schedule 15 of the Finance Act, 2003 applies where:

- A person transfers a chargeable interest (land) to the partnership; or

- A person transfers a chargeable interest (land) to a partnership and in return for that he or she receives an interest in the partnership (represented on their respective land capital account); or

- A person connected with either a partner or with a person who becomes a partner as a result of or in connection with the transfer of a chargeable interest (land) to the partnership.

So, in effect any case where the land becomes partnership property will be caught by these provisions. The charge itself is calculated by reference to the value of the land that is being treated as passing to the other partners. In other words, it is the proportion of value of the land which changes hands and it is that proportion of the market value of the interest which is charged to Stamp Duty Land Tax. The formula used is:

Market Value x (100 – Sum of the Lower Proportion) %

The calculation works by determining whether the person making the transfer is either a partner or is connected with a partner and working out what is the lowest of the percentage of their ownership of the land outside of the partnership against the percentage of their ownership (or that of connected persons) inside the partnership. Take the example of

Fred who transfers £1m value of land into a farming partnership with his son Adam and a family friend Richard. Each of them have a one-third income share in the partnership. The Stamp Duty Land Tax calculation is based on the amount of the value of the land now deemed to be owned (via the partnership) by the one unconnected person, Richard. This is measured by his one third share of income and so equates to £333,333. At a rate of 3% the tax charge will be £10,000.

For most farming partnerships, however, all of the partners are classed as connected persons. When all of the partners are connected to the person or persons transferring the land into the partnership and there is no consideration passing to the transferor, then there will be no Stamp Duty Land Tax payable. The calculation is only relevant when there is an unconnected partner in the partnership. So, in the above example if Richard were not a partner and it was just Fred and his daughter Alison then no Stamp Duty Land Tax would be payable. The statutory definition of who is and who is not a connected person comes from section 1122 of the Corporation Tax Act, 2010. This definition states that A is connected with B if A is a spouse of B, A is a relative of B, A is a spouse of a relative of B, A is a relative of B's spouse or A is the spouse of a relative of B's spouse. This can include a body of trustees. In relation to trusts the position varies between whether the Settlor of the trust is alive or not. Trustees who are in partnership with the Settlor are connected to him during his lifetime, but they cease to be connected once the Settlor has died.

11.2 Transfer of a partnership interest to another partner

Where the farm is held on the balance sheet of a partnership and there is an assignment of land capital between partners then no Stamp Duty Land Tax is payable unless the partnership is classed as a property investment partnership. For a majority of farming partnerships where the main activity is farming this should not be a difficulty. The definition of a property investment partnership for Stamp Duty Land Tax purposes is a partnership whose sole or main activity is investing or dealing in interests in land. For these purposes "sole or mainly" has the same meaning as "wholly or mainly" for Business Property Relief (section 105(3) of the Inheritance Tax Act, 1984). In a farming context it is therefore important to ensure that the trading activity undertaken on the farm is predominantly arising from trading agricultural activities rather than from perhaps diversified investment elements of the business such as cottages let on assured shorthold tenancies, holiday lets or rents from redundant farm barns which have been converted into business units.

11.3 Transfer of land from a partnership

The third instance when Stamp Duty Land Tax is relevant is when land is extracted from the farming partnership. This can happen when land is transferred from the partnership to a person who is or has been one of the partners of the partnership or to a person connected with a person who is or has been one of the partners of the partnership. The calculation is similar to that of bringing land into a partnership. A farming partnership holds land worth £10m allocated between the two senior partners George and Elizabeth in equal shares. Their children William, Harry and Margaret were brought into the partnership a few years ago. Each child has a 15% share of trading profits. Elizabeth wishes to take £2m worth of land out of the partnership. As all of the partners are connected, no stamp duty land tax is payable. But if William, Harry and Margaret were not Elizabeth's children but were instead her nephews and niece then the effect of the calculations of the sum of the lower proportions is that Stamp Duty Land Tax is payable on the share of the land value received by a partner which was previously attributed to partners who are not connected to Elizabeth. Therefore Stamp Duty Land Tax is payable on 45% of £2m.

11.4 The three year anti-avoidance rule

There is a very important anti-avoidance rule which can be a trap for unsuspecting partners. That is if land is extracted from a partnership within three years of it being transferred to the partnership then there will be a Stamp Duty Land Tax charge irrespective of whether consideration was given and (more importantly for farming partnerships) irrespective of whether the partners are all connected or not. If this happens then there is effectively a Stamp Duty Land Tax charge on the land originally introduced to the partnership. The other partners are treated as the purchasers for these purposes. These provisions may also be triggered even if the partner were to die within that three-year period. William introduces land into a partnership on 6 April 2018. On 29 September 2020 he dies and his personal representatives have the option of joining the partnership or withdrawing the land out of the partnership. If they were to do the latter then these anti-avoidance provisions would be triggered and Stamp Duty Land Tax would be payable. However, instead if the personal representatives joined the partnership and left William's capital in the partnership for the remainder of the three-year period before withdrawing the land then no Stamp Duty Land Tax would be payable.

CHAPTER TWELVE
IHT & CGT

Two of the most important taxes for farming partnerships are inheritance tax and capital gains tax. To understand why goes to the heart of the rationale for many farmers and landowners. That is the desire to pass on their farm or estate in a better condition than they inherited it. Not an easy task and one which often takes a lifetime of effort and hard work. At the core of the succession from one generation to the next is mitigating the capital taxes liability and family run partnerships can, if properly done, be a part of that process.

For inheritance tax there are two main reliefs to be borne in mind. Those are Agricultural Property Relief and Business Property Relief. Even if many professionals do not understand fully what is partnership property and what is not, most will be acutely aware of the key tax point that partnership property achieves 100% Business Property Relief for inheritance tax whilst land held outside of the partnership but used by the partnership only achieves 50% relief. For Agricultural Property Relief to apply the agricultural property needs to be occupied for agricultural purposes which can be challenging in a fully diversified farming business.

12.1 Agricultural Property Relief – the basics

Why bother with Agricultural Property Relief in a farming partnership context? For most businesses, Business Property Relief is surely the more relevant relief for inheritance tax purposes. There are two main reasons why Agricultural Property Relief still has a part to play for farming partnerships.

The first reason is what would happen if the claim for Business Property Relief fails? For example, the farm may have diversified into activities which are classed as being wholly or mainly investment activities such as let commercial property. The problem with Business Property Relief is that it is an all or nothing relief. Either the business qualifies or it does not. There is no halfway house. Having a claim for Agricultural Property Relief as well may mean that part of the farm still is able to qualify for relief from inheritance tax. The second reason is that Business Property Relief does not apply to the main house whereas it may qualify as a farmhouse for Agricultural Property Relief purposes.

The first question that must be asked is what elements of the farm qualify for agricultural property relief. This is defined by section 115(2) of the Inheritance Tax Act, 1984 as *"agricultural land or pasture and includes woodland and any other building used in connection with the intensive rearing of livestock or fish if the woodland or building is occupied with agricultural land or pasture and the occupation is ancillary to that of the agricultural land or pasture; and also includes such cottages, farm buildings and farmhouses, together with the land occupied with them, as are of a character appropriate to the property"*. When analysing a set of circumstances, it is often split the above definition into different sections. The first and most critical section is that there must be either agricultural land or pasture. If not, then no Agricultural Property Relief can be applied at all. The second section is woodland and intensive livestock or fish buildings occupied with the land and ancillary to that land. The third and final section is such farmhouses (not plural), cottages, and farm buildings (with land occupied with them) as are of a "character appropriate" to the property.

In order for agricultural property to qualify it must be occupied for the purposes of agriculture. There is no definition within the Inheritance Tax Act on what agricultural purposes means. However, HMRC's IHT manual (IHTM24061) does provide a helpful list of the activities that are recognised as agriculture. These are:

- Cultivation to produce food for human and animal consumption;

- Use of land to support livestock kept to produce food for human consumption, such as meat, milk or other products such as wool;

- The keeping of such other animals as may be found on an ordinary farm such as horses for farm work (not recreational);

- The breeding and grazing of racehorses on a stud farm;

- Land set aside for permanent or rotational fallow; and

- Cultivation of short rotation coppice.

Note that simply because an owner of a piece of land may qualify to receive a payment from the Rural Agency under the current Basic Payment Scheme or even, in future, the new Environmental Land Management Scheme (ELMS) does not in itself mean a claim for Agricultural Property would be successful.

Once you have satisfied yourselves that there is property which is being occupied for agricultural purposes then you need to ensure that the time periods as set out in section 117 of the Inheritance Tax Act, 1984 have been met. These are that you can apply for Agricultural Property Relief where:

- It was occupied by the transferor and used for the purposes of agriculture for the last two years (in hand farming) (s117(a)); or

- It was owned by the transferor and used for the purposes of agriculture for the last seven years (land let on a tenancy) (s117(b)).

In the context of farming partnerships a landowner who is also a partner in the farming business with the capital being held on his land capital account will need to satisfy the two year test (s117(a)) whereas a landowner who lets his land to a farming partnership under a formal tenancy arrangement will need to satisfy the seven year test (s117(b)). Occupation of land by a partnership is treated as occupation by the partners and this applies to each and every partner regardless of how active or inactive that partner may be in the business. This can be a helpful point when applying the occupation test to property farmed in partnership. Take the example of Rupert who had farmed the Farm for a number of years before bringing his wife, Alison, into partnership with him. The legal title to the land remained in Rupert's sole name and the partnership were allowed to occupy the land under licence. In 2019, Rupert retired from the partnership and his son, Andrew was admitted as a partner. In early 2020, Rupert transferred the land, half to his wife and half to his son. As Rupert was no longer occupying the land himself for the purposes of agriculture, having retired from the partnership, the transfer to Andrew would not satisfy the two-year occupation test under section 117(a) of the Inheritance Tax Act, 1984. Had he transferred the land whilst still a partner there would not have been a problem. However, the seven-year occupation test is satisfied by virtue of section 117(b) because throughout the relevant period up until the date of transfer the property had been occupied for the purposes of agriculture by the partnership of which Alison and Andrew were partners.

Finally, the actual test for the relief comes in section 116 of the Inheritance Tax Act, 1984 which in essence requires that for 100% Agricultural Property Relief to apply the transferor either has vacant possession of the property or can get it within 12 months. There is an Extra Statutory Concession (ESC F17) which extends the time limit to obtain vacant possession to 24 months. 100% relief also applies if there is a post 1 September 1995 agricultural tenancy including Agricultural Holdings Act tenancy successions and regrants after that date. The key point is that the ESC F17 concession only applies to tenanted agricultural land, not land subject to a licence. Therefore there can be a trap when the partnership agreement does not provide appropriate provisions to obtain vacant possession of the land and the land is being held under a mere licence. It follows that the partnership would be brought to an end on the retirement or death of a partner. However, following the case of *Harrison Broadley v Smith (1964) 1 WLR 464*, HMRC argue that in certain circumstances until the partnership can be determined, the landowner does not have vacant possession. This is on the basis that the landowner would not obtain vacant possession within 12 months from the date of death but from expiry of 12 months from the serving of the date of the notice. The simplest solution is to make sure there is a written partnership agreement in place with the appropriate provisions to give the landowner the right to vacant possession within the requisite 12 months.

It is important to note that Agricultural Property Relief applies to the agricultural value only and that may be different to the open market value. Agricultural value is defined in section 115(3) of the Inheritance Tax Act, 1984 as "*the value of the property if the property were subject to a perpetual covenant prohibiting its use otherwise than as agricultural property*". Any excess of value over and above the agricultural value will need to satisfy the tests for Business Property Relief.

12.2 More than one farmhouse

It is perfectly possible for a farming partnership to have more than farmhouse and the legislation does not restrict Agricultural Property Relief to one farmhouse. On the facts it could be shown that the farming operations are driven from more than one house. Nicola and Harriet inherit a large mixed farm operating both an arable and dairy business which they farm together under a partnership arrangement. However, when it comes to the day to day management and operation of the business Nicola concentrates her efforts on the dairy side whilst Harriet spends her time managing the arable side of the business. Both houses where Nicola and Harriet live could potentially qualify as farmhouses. For each farmhouse it is necessary to look at the bare land or pasture which is occupied with it to determine whether the farmhouse is of a character appropriate. The question to consider in such cases is whether the farming partnership business is of such a level that by its nature it is able to support the livelihood of the respective partners occupying the farmhouses, for which the relief is being claimed.

12.3 Haymaking and Partnerships

There is a Government trend to encourage activities in the Countryside to "enhance the natural environment" and the inference is that future subsidy payments under the new Environmental Land Management Scheme will encourage farmers further down this route. At the time of writing the details have yet to be worked out but it is easy to imagine this including such activities as cultivating wildflower meadows. The difficulty is that HMRC are taking an increasingly negative approach arguing that such activities does not qualify the land as being occupied for agricultural purposes and so denying the availability of Agricultural Property Relief. As a result there is currently a mismatch of policy between different government departments. One concern arising from this relates to those diversified farming partnership businesses which have moved away from traditional farming to haymaking with other letting activities. The view of practitioners is that a farmer who makes hay is a farmer and that whether that hay is ultimately consumed by livestock or by horses used for leisure purposes should not impact on the availability of Agricultural Property Relief. HMRC are beginning to put forward the argument that if the hay is sold for consumption of horses used for leisure purposes then that sale is not an agricultural activity in accordance with section 115 of the Inheritance Tax Act, 1984. The denying of Agricultural Property Relief in such cases presents a particular problem for farming partnerships where the land is held outside the partnership but is used by the partnership. The general tactic is to claim Business Property Relief at the rate of 50% and Agricultural Property Relief at the rate of 100%. The denying of the Agricultural Property Relief element means that only the 50% Business Property Relief would be available. In the case of *Personal Representatives of the estate of Vigne (deceased) v Revenue and Customs Comrs (2017) UKFTT 632 (TC)* the claim for Agricultural Property Relief on the hayfield failed because no hay crop was taken by the business in the two years prior to death.

12.4 Atkinson and the Ailing Farmer

Jack (the farmer) is nearing 78 and after a fall at home is absent from the farmhouse for a long period of convalescence before his death. As the house remained unoccupied during this period the availability of Agricultural Property Relief on the farmhouse is lost. With an ageing farming population this in not an uncommon scenario. Whether you are able to claim Agricultural Property Relief on the farmhouse will largely depend on the facts and the period of absence of the farmer. In the case of *Arnander & Ors (Executors of Mckenna dec'd) v Revenue & Customs Comrs (2006) Sp C 565* it was noted that "*neither Mr McKenna nor Lady Cecilia were able to engage in farming matters throughout the period of two years ending with the relevant dates of death"*. This is a moving test which is calculated back from the date of death and so Agricultural Property Relief can easily be lost on the Farmhouse if the farmer moves in residential care or hospital for any length of time.

A key advantage of farming partnerships in circumstances such as this is that occupation by a partnership of land is regarded as occupation of the land by all of the partners. This applies regardless of how active or inactive a particular partner is. To leave the house vacant for a long period is not a good idea. There is a need to put the farmhouse to an agricultural business use after the elderly farmer moves out. Perhaps with one of the more junior partners taking up residence.

The case of *Atkinson and Smith (Executors of the Will of William Atkinson (dec'd) v Revenue and Customs Comrs (2010) TC 420* concerned Mr Atkinson who had owned and occupied a bungalow. The farm had been let on an agricultural tenancy since 1980 to a partnership and Mr Atkinson remained a partner of that partnership until his death in 2006 with a 1% interest in the partnership capital. Due to ill health, however, in 2002 he moved out of the Bungalow and into a care home. During the next four years he visited the property and his possessions remained in the Bungalow. On his death, the executors claimed Agricultural Property Relief on the Bungalow.

The Upper Tribunal said that the correct approach was to identify a sufficient connection between the use and occupation of the bungalow and the agricultural activities being carried out by the partnership. Whilst Mr Atkinson occupied the bungalow before entering the care home there was sufficient connection. After that it cannot be said that he resided in the bungalow. His connection as partner and resident fell away and there needed to be a stronger connection between the use of the bungalow and the farming activities being undertaken for it to be held that the property was occupied for agricultural purposes.

The argument that the partnership was in occupation was rejected because the occupation was physically through Mr Atkinson as the person living there and not the partnership itself. The main function of the bungalow was to provide a home for Mr Atkinson.

It would have perhaps been a different result if the partnership held the land and house on the balance sheet of the partnership and the bungalow had been put to a business use during those four absent years.

12.5 Partnership Property, Capital Gains Tax and the Farmhouse

If a farm is being held jointly by the farming partners, then the strategy of what is to happen on a sale of the property needs to be considered from a practical viewpoint. Of particular importance is the restriction of Principal Private Residence Relief. The position is straightforward if there is only one residential property on the farm. Principal Private Residence Relief can be claimed by the partners in residence on the sale of the farm. But what would be the position if there is more than one residential property? Suppose you have a number of partners each of which live in a house on the farm. Those houses forming part of the land capital of the partnership. In accordance with section 59 of Taxation of Chargeable Gains Act, 1992 each partner is regarded for capital gains tax purposes as owning his fractional share of each of the chargeable assets owned by the partnership and the transactions carried on by the partnership are treated as dealings by the partners as individuals for capital gains tax purposes.

If there are, say, three partners, Tom, Dick and Harry and three properties which potentially could qualify for Principal Private Residence Relief, then the relief will be restricted to the gain on the sale of the farmhouse they live in. Effectively one third on each of the properties occupied. Thus Tom will only achieve Principal Private Residence Relief on one third of the house he lives in and Dick and Harry would be deemed to be taxed at 28% on the gain on that particular residence. The same treatment would apply for the treatment of the residences occupied by Dick and Harry. Potentially, it would be possible Dick and Harry to claim Entrepreneurs' Relief (now known as Business Asset Disposal Relief) reducing the rate to 10% or Rollover Relief if the proceeds are to be reinvested into a new farm. However, if you wish for

Tom, Dick and Harry to take full advantage of Principal Private Residence Relief then a possible solution to consider would be for the residential properties to be held outside of the partnership and each individual to become the sole owner of the property they live in. That way each of them will be able to claim Principal Private Residence Relief entirely on their respective residences.

12.6 Business property relief

As we have seen Agricultural Property Relief only applies to the agricultural value of the property whereas Business Property Relief is potentially available, in certain circumstances at the rate of 100% on the market value of the property. It therefore has a far greater potential when it comes to property and assets either owned by a partnership or used by a partnership.

Business Property Relief is a relief from inheritance tax on relevant business property which in a partnership context is either:

1. Property consisting of a business or an interest in a business (s105(1)(a), Inheritance Tax Act, 1984); or

2. Any land or building, machinery or plant which, immediately before the transfer, was used wholly or mainly for the purposes of a business carried on by a company of which the transferor then had control or by a partnership of which he then was a partner (s105(1)(d), Inheritance Tax Act, 1984).

A business includes a business carried on in the exercise of a profession or vocation and so is much wider than the term trade and can (as we shall see later) include some letting provided the business does not consist mainly of making or holding investments. Similar to the criteria for a formation of a partnership with a view of profit, the requirements for Business Property Relief exclude businesses that are not carried on for a gain (section 103(3) of Inheritance Tax Act, 1984) and hence hobby farming is unlikely to qualify.

An interest in a business will include a partner's share in a partnership. In other words, the capital which is credited to him in the partnership accounts. This could be both general capital and land capital and it is sufficient for the person to be a partner in the business. There is no requirement that the partner needs to be actively involved in the business in order to qualify. This can be extremely useful for more elderly farming partners who may physically not be able to work in the fields but are still involved within the partnership business. It can also include sleeping partners and part time partners.

A retired partner, however, cannot qualify for relief. In the case of *Beckman v IRC (2000) STC (SCD) 59* the deceased had retired from the partnership a number of years before she died. The deceased's capital account as a partner was derived from the capital introduced together with undrawn accumulated profits. At the time of her retirement her capital stood at £169,185 and at the time of her death four years later it was £112,811. The judge held that the deceased was a creditor of the business. It is therefore not an interest in a business and so the amount owed will not qualify for Business Property Relief.

12.7 Rates of Business Property Relief which apply to partnerships

The business or an interest in business under section 105(1)(a) of the Inheritance Tax Act, 1984 will qualify for relief at the rate of 100%. This will include property held on the capital account of the partnership and is one of the reasons why land is transferred to a partnership. Land and buildings owned outside of the partnership individually by one or more partners and used by the partnership will qualify for Business Property Relief at the rate of 50% (section 105(1)(d) of the Inheritance Tax Act, 1984). This is important because Agricultural Property Relief may not be available on all the property being used by the farming business, of if it does qualify, then the agricultural value is less than the open market value, for example, let cottages, farm buildings not in use for agricultural purposes or land with development potential (hope value). Transfers of partnership interests between partners will qualify for 100% relief.

Where the farming business is carried on by a partnership and the land is owned by a member of the partnership and let to is or the partnership is occupying it under licence then Agricultural Property Relief will apply at the rate of 100% and Business Property Relief will apply at the rate of 50% on the balance. If both reliefs are applied for then Agricultural Property Relief will always apply before Business Property Relief.

12.8 The mixed farming estate

Business Property Relief is denied to a business consisting wholly or mainly of the holding or making of investments. In a farming context this often comes up with former agricultural cottages which have subsequently been let on assured shorthold tenancies to third parties but it also relevant to other diversified activities which mainly consist of collecting rent. An example would be redundant farm buildings which have been converted into office accommodation. However, following the vase of *Farmer & Giles v ITC (1999) STC (SCD) 321* the cottages in the farming partnership were held to qualify for Business Property Relief because they were fully integrated into the farming trading business and the letting activities were not significant. Various factors were considered in relation to the farming and the letting activities. This included the value of capital employed, the time spent in labour, the turnover, the net profits and the overall feel of the business in the round.

This decision was reinforced in the case of *Brander (representative of James (dec'd), Fourth Earl of Balfour) v Revenue and Customs Comrs (2009) UKFTT 101 (TC)* where Lord Balfour entered into a farming partnership with his nephew in 2002. He died in 2003 and HMRC contested that Business Property Relief was not applicable because the investment activities of the Estate were significant. Applying the principles in Farmer & Giles, the Tribunal held that the estate did qualify for Business Property Relief. Interesting HMRC also argued that the partnership had been in existence for less then two years and so Business Property Relief did not apply in accordance with the provisions of section 106 of the Inheritance Tax Act, 1984. The personal representatives contended that the effect of the replacement provisions under section 107 of the Inheritance Tax Act, 1984 meant that the estate did qualify as the interest of the deceased in the partnership replaced the business which he previously had carried on as a beneficiary of a family settlement. The Tribunal agreed with the personal representatives.

12.9 Capital Gains Tax and Partnerships

Like other taxes, the Capital Gains Tax rules look through a partnership and treat each partner individually. Any dealings are treated as dealings by the individual partners and not the partnership. For tax purposes a partnership is no more that a collection of separate persons and, in accordance with section 59 of the Taxation of Chargeable Gains Act, 1992 each partner is regarded for capital gains tax purposes as owning his or her fractional share of each of the assets of the partnership.

Statement of Practice D12 states that partners are treated as owning fractional shares in the partnership's assets. It explains that there is a disposal for the purposes of tax on chargeable gains if either the partnership disposes of an asset or there is a change in the partnership's capital sharing ratio. This would include changes that would arise on the retirement or admission of a partner.

HMRC Brief 03/08 concerned the position when a partner introduces land into the partnership to be held by them on land capital accounts. HMRC take the view that the contributing partner has made a part disposal of the asset equal to the fractional share which passes to the other partners. This means they will apply the statutory A/A+B formula which is likely to give rise to a chargeable gain. However, if the asset contributed (land) is credited 100% to the capital account of that partner who has introduced it into the partnership then there would be no disposal at all and so no tax event for capital gains tax purposes. There is a school of thought, however, that if one particular asset is credited 100% to that partner's capital account then there hasn't been any capital contribution by that partner merely that the partner is allowing the partnership to use that asset. For this reason it is usually recommended that a small portion is credited to the other partners, say 5%, to avoid this question arising.

12.10 Business Asset Disposal Relief (Entrepreneurs' Relief)

Each partner who has a partnership share for at least two years may be able to claim business asset disposal relief where he disposes of all or part of his interest in the partnership or the partnership disposes of all or part of a business carried on by it, or a disposal by the partner of an asset used by the partnership in its business as part of his withdrawal from the business or he disposes of an asset used by the partnership. For the latter to work it will depend on the associated disposal rules and the partner must have at least a 5% interest in the business. This relief allows business owners to benefit from a reduced rate of capital gains tax at 10% on the first £1m of gains. It is a lifetime limit and so any previous claim will be counted in the lifetime limit.

For the claim to succeed there has to be a disposal of the business or part of it. A claim for the relief failed in the farming partnership case of *Russell v Revenue and Customs Comrs (2012) UKFTT 623 (TC)* where some land it held was sold for development because it was considered that there had not been a disposal of a business. The only impact on the farming business was that the profits generated would be lower.

Whilst the limit has been reduced from £10m to £1m in recent years, this relief can still be advantageous for farming business. Take the example of Bill who has owned a joint share in some land for many years. At various times, it has been rented to several farmers, but Bill and his co-owners have never farmed the land themselves. There is now a potential for development on the land. Faced with this, Bill could form a partnership with his co-owners and bring the land onto the balance sheet. The partnership would need to farm the land themselves or undertake the farming activity through a contract farming arrangement with a local farmer. After at least two years of trading activity it would be possible to wind up the business and claim business asset disposal relief on the disposal of the land.

12.11 Holdover Relief

If a partner disposes of all or part of their interest in the farming partnership by way of gift then holdover relief may be available under section 165 of the Taxation of Chargeable Gains Act, 1992. Care needs to be taken to ensure that the claim is made correctly and on time. It can also apply where the farmland is owned by a partner but let or made available to the farming business. This is on the basis that the partner has owned the farmland for at least seven years and throughout that period it has been occupied for the purposes of agriculture. As such it qualifies for Agricultural Property Relief and so you are able to holdover the gain using section 165 of the Taxation of Chargeable Gains Act, 1992.

12.12 Rollover Relief

It is also possible for a partner in a farming partnership to secure rollover relief under section 152 of the Taxation of Chargeable Gains Act, 1992 on a disposal of an interest and the acquisition of a new qualifying asset. To secure the relief an individual partner needs to show he had an interest in both the old assets and in the new. For farming partnership this usually takes the form of land held on the land capital account. It is the share of his interest in the partnership which is important rather then a share in income profits. This can be particularly useful if you have a partner who has very little active involvement in the business and consequently a small entitlement to income profits but has credited to him in the land capital account a large proportion of the underlying land. This partner will still be able to secure full rollover relief on a replacement asset. The position would be different if he had fully retired from the partnership.

For land held outside of the farming partnership but used by the partnership, then the freehold owners themselves cannot claim the relief. However, if the owners are also partners in the business, then they can claim rollover relief, irrespective of whether the partnership pays a rent for the farmland or they allow the partnership to occupy the land under licence for no consideration.

12.13 Farmhouses and Rollover Relief

CG 60990 of HMRC's Capital Gains Manual states that *"a house provided by a partnership for occupation as the private residence of a partner may qualify for relief"* under section 155 of the Taxation of Chargeable Gains Act, 1992 if:

- *"The terms of the partnership agreement require the particular partner to live in the particular house; or*

- *The occupation of the house by the partner is essential to the trade of the partnership"*

This is a relevant provision for many farms where at least one of the partners lives in the farmhouse. Of course, the sale of a farmhouse itself will not usually cause any issues because in most cases principal main residence relief (section 222 of the Taxation of Chargeable Gains Act, 1992) will apply for the partner occupying the property. But what if there is a gain on the farmland and it is the proceeds of sale from that land which are used to purchase a farmhouse for use of a partner? Would rollover relief be available by the other partners? The manual suggests that it will be available if the conditions are met and so it would seem sensible to include within the partnership agreement a requirement for the partner to live at the farmhouse or to live on the farm and at the farmhouse.

12.14 Partitions of Joint Interests in Land

Tom and John (brothers) have been farming in partnership for a number of years. They hold Manor Farm jointly 50/50 on their respective land capital accounts. In other words, no one part of the farm is held 100% by either of them. This means that if Tom and John sell a cottage in the partnership and there has been no transfer of interests so that they hold it together then each will be regarded as disposing of a 50% share and will be taxed accordingly on the gain arising. For each individual property both Tom and John have an undivided 50% interest and in order for one partner to own one particular property and so benefit from the entire proceeds then there would have to be a disposal by one partner and an acquisition by the other of that share. HMRC's treatment of changes in partnership interests are set out in the Statement of Practice D12. The key aspects of Statement D12 (as revised in September 2015) are:

- each partner is treated as owning a fractional share of each partnership asset; and

- a partner makes a disposal when:

    o the partnership disposes of the asset; or

    o his fractional share in the asset is reduced.

Since both Tom and John are connected the disposal consideration will be a fraction (equal to the fractional share changing hands) of the current balance sheet value of the asset and tax would be payable on that change by the donor. The donee will not realise a chargeable gain, instead the tax cost will be the property's market value as at the date of the gift reduced by the donee's gain. However, where there is an exchange of interests, for example Tom's interest in Elderflower Cottage is exchanged for John's interest in Rose Cottage both interests being valued at £170,000 then we can take advantage of section 248A of the Taxation of Chargeable Gains Act, 1992. This offers a modified form of rollover relief and applies to all land, even when not used for the purposes of a trade. The effect of this section is that both Tom and John can exchange their interests in the properties and provided the exchange of interests is of equal value there would be no capital gains tax payable. In other words, the joint operation of Statement of Practice D12 and s248A of the Taxation of the Chargeable Gains Act, 1992 assist in deferring capital gains tax on the reorganisation of the partnership. Furthermore, once a particular parcel of land is held 100% in one partner's land capital account it is possible for that property to be withdrawn from the partnership by that partner without triggering a capital gains tax disposal. If that partner were to subsequently dispose of the property to a third-party then the base value for capital gains tax purposes would be the base value of when the property was acquired by John/Tom and tax payable on the gain from that date.

12.15 Gifts with reservation of benefit

Care is needed that the Gift of Reservation of Benefit provisions do not apply in connection with lifetime gifts of farm property, particularly where that land forms part of the farm partnership which includes the donor and the donor wishes to retain a profit share in the partnership which exceeds his entitlement under his respective capital account.

CHAPTER THIRTEEN
THE USE OF LIMITED PARTNERSHIPS AND LIMITED LIABILITY PARTNERSHIPS

Most farming partners farm under a partnership governed by the Partnership Act, 1890 but there are occasions when a partnership with limited liability for the partners is more appropriate.

13.1 Limited Partnerships

The law governing Limited Partnerships is still governed by the Partnerships Act, 1890 but as modified by the Limited Partnerships Act, 1907 and supplemented by the Limited Partnerships (Forms) Rules, 2009. As with an ordinary traditional partnership, a limited partnership is not recognised as a legal entity in its own right.

The Limited Partnership works in very much the same ways as a traditional partnership. There has to be one or more general partners who has unlimited liability and it is the unlimited partners who have the management of the partnership. The difference is that it is also possible for one or more partners to join into the partnership but their liability is only limited to the capital they have actually introduced.

The other difference with a Limited Partnership is that certain details have to be registered at Companies House. These include:

- The partnership's name;
- The nature of the business;
- The principal place of business;
- The full name of each partner;

- The date of commencement of the partnership;

- A statement that it is a limited partnership; and

- Particulars of each limited partner, including the amount contributed to the partnership (whether by way of cash, land, deadstock or livestock).

Importantly there is no requirement to file annual accounts. It therefore has more confidentiality than a Limited Liability Partnership and appeals to many farmers who do not wish their profits or losses to be made public knowledge. Failure to register the above details or any change to them will render the limited liability ineffective.

13.2 Use of Limited Partnerships in a farming context

Suppose a farmer wishes to bring his children into the farming business after his death but is concerned that if he dies in the next few years they would be too young and inexperienced to take on the full mantle of responsibility. In the light of this he decides in his Will to have a discretionary trust and to appoint his accountant and his lawyer (as the family's trusted advisors) as trustees. His primary wish in the letter of wishes, which accompanies his Will, is for the farming business to continue with his children involved but also for the trustees to have a guiding hand. One way to perhaps achieve this is through a Limited Partnership, where the trustees' liability would be limited to the value of the partnership assets. This gives the professional executors/trustees comfort that by taking on the role of partner they are not exposing their own personal assets to any liabilities of the business. It also gives the farmer the comfort that after he is gone the children will have the ability to call on or have access to the skill set which the professional trustees can bring to the arrangement.

It is, of course, important that the trustees have the relevant powers under the trust deed or Will to take on that role. So, if such an arrangement is being complemented then as part of those discussions it is critical that the trust provisions are checked.

13. USE OF LIMITED PARTNERSHIPS & LIMITED LIABILITY PARTNERSHIPS • 149

The other main use of Limited Partners in a farming context is to involve non-farming members in the farming business, particularly if they have an interest in the underlying land. Take the example of Pippa, Tom and Daniel. Following the death of their father, Harry, the family farm was left in equal shares to his three children. The siblings get on well together but it is only Daniel who is actively interested in farming. Are they storing up trouble for the future if there is no agreement to regulate their arrangements? Both Pippa and Tom have careers away from the farm but they still wish to feel involved in the farm and to protect their inheritance tax position on their respective deaths. A Limited Partnership allows Pippa and Tom to be limited partners in the partnership and so feel involved as stakeholders but they are not involved with the day to day management of the farm. This is left to Daniel as the unlimited partner. This arrangement meets Daniel's wishes to be left alone to farm and also Pippa's and Tom's wishes to maximise the Agricultural Property Relief and Business Property Relief position in the event of their deaths. Effectively, Pippa and Tom as stakeholders would be sleeping partners and this will allow Daniel to manage and run the farm.

13.3 Forfeiture of limited liability

There are three instances in which a limited partner may face liability for the debts and obligations of the partnership beyond the amount he or she originally contributed.

- The partnership's details (or any changes to them) have not been registered as required;

- A limited partner takes part in the management of the partnership business; and

- A limited partner draws out any part of his contribution.

If the advantages of Limited Partnership is to succeed then it is critical that the limited partners do not take part in the three instances outlined above. The greatest risk will be the limited partner becoming involved in the day to day management of the partnership business. This may happen gradually over time and until there is a blurring of lines. Therefore the roles of each of the partners and what they should be doing should be reviewed and clarified on a regular basis.

13.4 Limited Liability Partnerships

Probably the most familiar type of partnerships for professionals (because most professional service partnerships are them) are Limited Liability Partnerships. There are 59,000 registered Limited Liability Partnerships in the UK but ironically there are far less common for our agricultural clients. Technically they are not even a partnership in the truest sense but a body corporate with members instead of partners. A sort of hybrid between a company and a partnership. Section 1(5) of the Limited Liability Partnership Act, 2000 expressly excludes most partnership law from applying and so Limited Liability Partnerships have more in common with Company Law then Partnership Law. The Partnership Act, 1890 does not apply to Limited Liability Partnerships. In other words, the approach is devised from applied company law with distinct partnership elements. Unlike a company, however, there are no directors, shareholders or share capital. In general terms a member of the Limited Liability Partnership is liable only to the extent of the capital introduced and undrawn profits.

There is a gap of 110 years between the Partnership Act, 1890 and the Limited Liability Partnership Act, 2000. During that period and even before a considerable amount of case law has been built up which deals with issues which are either not covered by statute or provides clarification of particular provisions. The Limited Liability Partnership does not have that resource and therefore one is very much reliant on the provisions of the 2000 Act. It is, therefore, even more important that the agreement governing the Limited Liability Partnership has within it all of the provisions required for it to be of practical use in a farming context. This will require a good understanding of the underlying business as most precedents are prepared with professional service partnerships in mind any standard agreement will need substantial alteration.

In one particular respect this ensuring that the agreement is fit for purpose is very important; that is on the provisions relating to a partner (member) leaving the Limited Liability Partnership. Unlike an ordinary partnership unless the agreement so specifies there is no entitlement for the deceased or retiring partner to the repayment of capital and to a share of the surplus value of assets. Without adequate provisions, the capital could potentially accrue to the other members and any capital profits will remain within the Limited Liability Partnership until such time as it is appropriated.

13.5 Use of Limited Liability Partnerships in a farming context

Where they arise in an agricultural context is where the business, in whole or in part, has an element of high risk and the client wishes to limit the risk to the assets within the partnership. A good example of this in a landed estate context would be the running of an aerodrome, which potentially has a high risk of liability if things go wrong. Therefore a separate Limited Liability Partnership is drawn up in which the land occupied by the aerodrome is placed on the balance sheet. Any liability arising is therefore limited to the land and other assets of the Limited Liability Partnership. The rest of the estate is run entirely separately under an ordinary farming partnership.

CHAPTER FOURTEEN
INCOME TAX

There are many good books on the market on the income tax treatment of partnerships and there is little point in just repeating those. This chapter is therefore highlighting the basics which need to be taken into account and those areas where case law affects specifically farming partnerships.

It is a rare occurrence for a farmer to admit that he makes a decent profit from farming, but some do, and that achievement is all the more remarkable when you reflect on all the changes a farmer faces in the modern market. When it comes to taxation items of an income nature are subject to income tax and this is the same whether you are an individual or in partnership with others.

Potentially problematic for farmers is Making Tax Digital. This is a highly complex area with stock valuations including the herd basis, farmer's averaging of profits and seasonal fluctuations which means to arrive at a partnership's profit or loss includes a number of adjustments unique to the farming industry. That is why an accountant with the appropriate knowledge and experience of agriculture and farming are worth the professional fees they are charging.

14.1 Farming income as a trade

Income tax is an annual tax, annually re-imposed by Parliament. As farming is treated as a trade for income tax purposes, so therefore the profits from the farming business, whether it is managed on a commercial basis or not, are taxed as trading income. Section 996, Income Tax Act, 2007 defines farming as *"the occupation of land wholly or mainly for the purposes of husbandry, but does not include market gardening"*. This definition has further been clarified by case law to include activities appropriate to land recognisable as farmland and involve the raising of livestock, cultivating land and growing crops. Commercial woodlands are not a trade for income tax purposes.

All of the farming activities carried on by the farming partnership are treated as one trade. This is the case even if there were several farms and in different parts of the UK.

14.2 The taxation of profits of a farming partnership

As farming partnerships are not separate legal entities, they are not taxed themselves on their profits. Partnerships are often described as transparent for tax purposes and this is the reason why. Instead individual partners are assessed for income tax purposes on their respective share of the partnership profits. This is achieved through a two-stage process. The first stage is for the partnership to calculate its taxable profit or loss using the tax rules which apply. Once this has been established, then the second stage is to allocate a share of that profit or loss to each partner in accordance with the profit sharing provisions within the partnership agreement. The individual partner then includes their share of the profits or losses in their own personal tax return and pay the tax accordingly.

There are statutory provisions dealing with disputes between partners concerning profit shares. This enables any partner to refer the allocation of profits to the tax tribunal. This must be done within a twelve-month time limit from submission of the tax return, or from an amendment to a return.

14.3 Expenditure of a capital or income nature

In order to calculate trading profits, there is a need to deduct from the gross trading receipts, the expenses of an income nature. The general rule is that expenditure of a capital nature is not deductible for income tax purposes. Nor can you deduct expenses not incurred wholly and exclusively for the purposes of the trade or losses not connected with or arising out of the trade.

In relation to expenditure of a capital nature, the obvious question to ask is what does this mean in practice? There is no comprehensive list of what is capital expenditure but there are a number of tests arising out of case law which assists. In summary:

- Capital expenditure has a once and for all quality to it;

- Was it done with a view to bringing into existence an asset or advantage for the enduring benefit of the trade; and

- Was the expenditure laid out on the creation, acquisition, improvement or modification of a fixed asset such as a farm building (so capital in nature) or on the maintenance and repair of an asset (income in nature).

The point is well demonstrated in the farming partnership case of *G Pratt & Sons v Revenue and Customs Comrs (TC01269) (2011) UKFTT 416 (TC)* where the partnership claimed a deduction for the cost of £23,300 for resurfacing a farm driveway. HMRC argued that the concreting of the driveway had provided a new and better surface and therefore this was an improvement to the original driveway rather then merely a repair or maintenance of one. The partners argued that the new surface had been laid over the existing surface, filling in potholes and generally creating a hard-core base on the original stone. It was therefore simply a repair. The First Tier Tribunal agreed with the partnership.

The question came up again in the case of *Cairnsmill Caravan Park v Revenue and Customs Comrs (TC02580) (2013) UKFTT 164 (TC)*. This related to the replacement of the grass surface of a caravan park by a hard-core surface and the Tribunal agreed that the cost of the hard care surface was correctly treated as an expenditure of an income nature. What these cases show is that it is important to have a good understanding of what work has been undertaken and the value both before and after. With this information you then need to measure any enhancement and improvement element of the works and, if required, produce evidence of the lack of improvement to the farming entity.

14.4 Profit averaging

The system of averaging farming profits has been around for over forty years and with effect from the 2016/17 tax year, farmers now have the choice as to whether they average their profits over five years, two years or not at all. In essence it is a tax relief that enables a farming partnership to make an averaging claim where their trading income profits fluctuate from year to year. In other words, it adjusts the amount of profits for each of the tax years to which the claim relates in order to reduce the variation between them.

The uncertainty around Brexit and milder and wet winters has produced a great variance in profits for many farmers over recent years and so the system of averaging may be a useful device to reduce the fluctuations in profits. Take the example of Philip, John and Harriet who had farmed in partnership for a number of years. Harriet's share of the farming partnership profit amount to £100,000. The profits in previous tax years had been lower due to losses and some substantial capital expenditure. By taking the opportunity to average the year with the previous four years meant that most of the profits were taxed at basic rates and all the personal allowances for the family were utilised. This not only reduced the tax liability substantially it also assisted in reducing the tax payments on account which benefited the partnership's cash flow position.

It could be said that a lot of farming partnerships already operate their own informal averaging of farm profit by tax efficient profit-sharing percentage through the family who are also partners in the business. In a partnership agreement there is often a provision that the profits and losses each year can be varied between themselves as partners with agreement. This would be done at a partners' meeting and recorded in the minutes. If profit shares are altered then it is important that the correct documentation is in place such as the partnership minutes and accounts as well as ensuring that HMRC have been reported the correct information.

An averaging claim can be made if either:

- The profits for one of the two tax years is less than 75% of the other (for a two-year claim) or the average profits over the first four tax years to which the claim relates are less than 75% of the profits in the fifth tax year (for a five-year claim); or

- No profits have been made in one or more (but not all) of the tax years over the relevant period.

An averaging claim cannot be made in the year of commencement or on a cessation of the business. This includes partners joining or leaving an existing partnership in a particular year. Nor can you include a tax year preceding a tax year that has already been included in an averaging claim. Each individual partner may make an averaging claim in respect of their own share of the partnership profits. This therefore gives the ability of allowing more longstanding partners still to claim even if the newer partners have only recently been admitted and are unable to do so.

Only pure farming trades centred in the UK including the intensive rearing of livestock or fish on a commercial basis for the production of food for human consumption may average profits. Excluded are farm contractors and businesses where the farming is just part of a larger trade that includes substantial non-farming activities.

If the intention is to make a claim then it is important to plan ahead and ensure the correct procedure is followed. This includes making sure that all the tax and accounts information is available for the relevant period and in respect of the accounts they have been agreed and signed by all of the partners. Check also that the partnership agreement gives the power to vary the profits as they shall determine year on year and if the profit sharing ratios have been varied then that the correct amounts have been reported in the tax returns of the individual partners, and recorded in the accounts and partnership minutes.

14.5 Farm losses and sideways loss relief

Any losses are divided in accordance with the Partnership Agreement and like profits, the share of the losses created is personal to that partner. This can be disadvantageous if losses are allocated to a partner without other income, instead of a partner with investment income, which can be reclaimed by applying farming losses.

It is possible for a partner accruing a trading loss for income tax purposes, to make a claim to offset that loss from their other net income in the current tax year and the previous tax year. Farmers are subject to additional restrictions on the application of this relief. These are that if either of the following applies the relief is denied:

- The business was not run on a commercial basis with a view to making a profit; or

- They incurred losses before capital allowances in each of the five preceding tax years (the hobby-farming restriction).

In the case of *French v Revenue and Customs Comrs (TC04053) (2014) UKFTT 940 (TC)*, the husband and wife had farmed since 1961. Originally an arable farm, they changed to dairy in 1968 but after the livestock was sold in 2000, the farm switched back to arable and was farmed under contract by a neighbour until 2004. At this point Mr and Mrs French took the farm back in hand and farmed as a partnership. The partnership employed a contractor but the business continued to make losses until 2011/12 tax year when it returned a profit. HMRC denied loss relief on the basis that there had been thirteen years of losses recorded. The Tribunal agreed with Mr and Mrs French however, that they had not farmed during the 2000-2004 period and consequently there had only been six years of losses. They were considered to be competent commercial farmers and allowed a break from farming. The case demonstrates the need to have the relevant evidence to hand and in cases such as the above, a correct legal analysis of the documentation relating to the farming business, as HMRC are likely to question the availability of this relief.

For the purposes of the hobby farming restriction, the loss is computed before capital allowances and is taken up to 5 April each year. Any start up business is likely to incur losses during its first year and farming is no different. For this reason the first year of losses are ignored. This means that where a new farming business makes consecutive losses, it is the loss on the seventh tax year and not the sixth tax year which will be caught. A point demonstrated in the French case above as the creation of the farm partnership in 2004 was treated as a new business. As soon as the business has made a profit then the chain of losses is broken and the five year rule will not apply again until they have subsequently been a further five years of losses.

The case of Michael E Robins v Revenue and Customs Comrs (TC02902) (2014) UKFTT 514 (TC) demonstrated the importance of quantifying the loss claim being made. In this case Mr Robins received income from a farming partnership and from a haulage business. The 2010/11 tax return was submitted on time and assessed as having tax payable in January 2012. However, the 2011/12 tax return submitted in May 2012 showed losses including a claim to carry back the losses for the 2010/11 period. Whilst the accountant had written stating that there was an intention to make a claim for loss relief for the 2010/11 tax year and that was why the tax due for that year had not been paid, HMRC argued that the letter was not valid as the losses had not been quantified.

14.6 Reporting issues when there is a partnership dispute

Sadly, it is quite possible that individual partners will dispute aspects of the treatment of the partnership business accounts and tax. This in turn could lead to HMRC issuing penalties to individual partners even when the reason for a delay in reporting is due to the fact that the partnership has not provided the appropriate figures to put on the tax return. In the case of Gavin *Faulkner v HMRC (2018) TC6500* the First Tier Tribunal agreed that the inability of a member of a Limited Liability Partnership to obtain figures for a loss claim could be a reasonable excuse for late filing. Mr Faulkner was a member of a loss-making partnership and wished to use the losses to set against his other income. Unfortunately, he could not get the amount of loss quantified from third parties. He did notify HMRC several times about the problem and he finally received information about the losses in 2006/7 tax year in 2012. The Tribunal had no powers to require HMRC to allow a late claim but given the letters to HMRC and its poor handling of the case, the judge hoped that HMRC would reconsider. It also commented that it had no powers when a partner is required to do the impossible.

The acceptance of reasonable excuse was also given in the case of *Porter v The Commissioner for Revenue and Customs (2016) UK FTT 401* which involved the late submission of the farming partnership return. In this case Mr and Mrs Porter were partners in the business. Mrs Porter was not the nominated partner and had been excluded from the management of the business during an acrimonious divorce with her husband. She was not made aware that the return had not been filed until after the submission deadline and it was reasonable for her to have assumed that the partnership accountant had filed the return upon direction by her ex-husband.

As well as individual partners not being given access to the appropriate figures there can be times when there is a disagreement between partners as to the correct amount of profit share or loss which is being allocated to them. This could arise from not having the appropriate written partnership agreement in place, an inadequately drafted partnership agreement or a disagreement over the accounting assumptions. The latter could be, for example, a dispute over the amount of private use of a business asset.

Following the Morgan and Self cases, HMRC take the view that the partners should attempt to resolve the differences between themselves but that where there is a genuine disagreement that cannot be resolved then HMRC's published guidance (EM7025) states that *"individual partners should:*

- *Enter, as their share of partnership profits, the amount they consider to be correct; and*

- *Advise us that they have done so by making an entry in the white space notes section of the return to show*

  - *The profits as allocated in the partnership statement*

  - *The deduction (or addition) of the disputed amount, and*

  - *An explanation about why they think the profit allocated to them in the partnership statement is wrong*

On this basis HMRC will not regard the personal return as incorrect, but the guidance does note that each case will turn on its facts. Far better to enter negotiations with the co-partners and agree an allocation of profits/losses. Where there is a dispute within the partnership, then it is a good idea for separate advisors for each of the partners to be instructed and that all of the partners receive details of draft accounts and queries and are kept updated on filing deadlines. All these cases show the complexity surrounding partnership accounts and tax returns and the need to ensure that they reflect what the partners agree.

MORE BOOKS BY LAW BRIEF PUBLISHING

A selection of our other titles available now:-

'Covid-19, Homeworking and the Law – The Essential Guide to Employment and GDPR Issues' by Forbes Solicitors
'Covid-19, Force Majeure and Frustration of Contracts – The Essential Guide' by Keith Markham
'Covid-19 and Criminal Law – The Essential Guide' by Ramya Nagesh
'Covid-19 and Family Law in England and Wales – The Essential Guide' by Safda Mahmood
'Covid-19 and the Implications for Planning Law – The Essential Guide' by Bob Mc Geady & Meyric Lewis
'Covid-19, Residential Property, Equity Release and Enfranchisement – The Essential Guide' by Paul Sams and Louise Uphill
'Covid-19, Brexit and the Law of Commercial Leases – The Essential Guide' by Mark Shelton
'Covid-19 and the Law Relating to Food in the UK and Republic of Ireland – The Essential Guide' by Ian Thomas
'A Practical Guide to the General Data Protection Regulation (GDPR) – 2nd Edition' by Keith Markham
'Ellis on Credit Hire – Sixth Edition' by Aidan Ellis & Tim Kevan
'A Practical Guide to Working with Litigants in Person and McKenzie Friends in Family Cases' by Stuart Barlow
'Protecting Unregistered Brands: A Practical Guide to the Law of Passing Off' by Lorna Brazell
'A Practical Guide to Secondary Liability and Joint Enterprise Post-Jogee' by Joanne Cecil & James Mehigan

'A Practical Guide to the Pre-Action RTA Claims Protocol for Personal Injury Lawyers' by Antonia Ford
'A Practical Guide to Neighbour Disputes and the Law' by Alexander Walsh
'A Practical Guide to Forfeiture of Leases' by Mark Shelton
'A Practical Guide to Coercive Control for Legal Practitioners and Victims' by Rachel Horman
'A Practical Guide to Rights Over Airspace and Subsoil' by Daniel Gatty
'Tackling Disclosure in the Criminal Courts – A Practitioner's Guide' by Narita Bahra QC & Don Ramble
'A Practical Guide to the Law of Driverless Cars – Second Edition' by Alex Glassbrook, Emma Northey & Scarlett Milligan
'A Practical Guide to TOLATA Claims' by Greg Williams
'Artificial Intelligence – The Practical Legal Issues' by John Buyers
'A Practical Guide to the Law of Prescription in Scotland' by Andrew Foyle
'A Practical Guide to the Construction and Rectification of Wills and Trust Instruments' by Edward Hewitt
'A Practical Guide to the Law of Bullying and Harassment in the Workplace' by Philip Hyland
'How to Be a Freelance Solicitor: A Practical Guide to the SRA-Regulated Freelance Solicitor Model' by Paul Bennett
'A Practical Guide to Prison Injury Claims' by Malcolm Johnson
'A Practical Guide to the Small Claims Track' by Dominic Bright
'A Practical Guide to Advising Clients at the Police Station' by Colin Stephen McKeown-Beaumont
'A Practical Guide to Antisocial Behaviour Injunctions' by Iain Wightwick
'Practical Mediation: A Guide for Mediators, Advocates, Advisers, Lawyers, and Students in Civil, Commercial, Business, Property, Workplace, and Employment Cases' by Jonathan Dingle with John Sephton
'The Mini-Pupillage Workbook' by David Boyle

'A Practical Guide to Crofting Law' by Brian Inkster
'A Practical Guide to Spousal Maintenance' by Liz Cowell
'A Practical Guide to the Law of Domain Names and Cybersquatting' by Andrew Clemson
'A Practical Guide to the Law of Gender Pay Gap Reporting' by Harini Iyengar
'A Practical Guide to the Rights of Grandparents in Children Proceedings' by Stuart Barlow
'NHS Whistleblowing and the Law' by Joseph England
'Employment Law and the Gig Economy' by Nigel Mackay & Annie Powell
'A Practical Guide to Noise Induced Hearing Loss (NIHL) Claims' by Andrew Mckie, Ian Skeate, Gareth McAloon
'An Introduction to Beauty Negligence Claims – A Practical Guide for the Personal Injury Practitioner' by Greg Almond
'Intercompany Agreements for Transfer Pricing Compliance' by Paul Sutton
'Zen and the Art of Mediation' by Martin Plowman
'A Practical Guide to the SRA Principles, Individual and Law Firm Codes of Conduct 2019 – What Every Law Firm Needs to Know' by Paul Bennett
'A Practical Guide to Adoption for Family Lawyers' by Graham Pegg
'A Practical Guide to Industrial Disease Claims' by Andrew Mckie & Ian Skeate
'A Practical Guide to Redundancy' by Philip Hyland
'A Practical Guide to Vicarious Liability' by Mariel Irvine
'A Practical Guide to Applications for Landlord's Consent and Variation of Leases' by Mark Shelton
'A Practical Guide to Relief from Sanctions Post-Mitchell and Denton' by Peter Causton
'A Practical Guide to Equity Release for Advisors' by Paul Sams
'A Practical Guide to Unlawful Eviction and Harassment' by Stephanie Lovegrove
'A Practical Guide to the Law Relating to Food' by Ian Thomas

'A Practical Guide to Financial Services Claims' by Chris Hegarty
'The Law of Houses in Multiple Occupation: A Practical Guide to HMO Proceedings' by Julian Hunt
'A Practical Guide to Unlawful Eviction and Harassment' by Stephanie Lovegrove
'A Practical Guide to Solicitor and Client Costs' by Robin Dunne
'Occupiers, Highways and Defective Premises Claims: A Practical Guide Post-Jackson – 2nd Edition' by Andrew Mckie
'A Practical Guide to Financial Ombudsman Service Claims' by Adam Temple & Robert Scrivenor
'A Practical Guide to Advising Schools on Employment Law' by Jonathan Holden
'A Practical Guide to Running Housing Disrepair and Cavity Wall Claims: 2nd Edition' by Andrew Mckie & Ian Skeate
'A Practical Guide to Holiday Sickness Claims – 2nd Edition' by Andrew Mckie & Ian Skeate
'Arguments and Tactics for Personal Injury and Clinical Negligence Claims' by Dorian Williams
'A Practical Guide to QOCS and Fundamental Dishonesty' by James Bentley
'A Practical Guide to Drone Law' by Rufus Ballaster, Andrew Firman, Eleanor Clot
'A Practical Guide to Compliance for Personal Injury Firms Working With Claims Management Companies' by Paul Bennett
'A Practical Guide to the Landlord and Tenant Act 1954: Commercial Tenancies' by Richard Hayes & David Sawtell
'A Practical Guide to Dog Law for Owners and Others' by Andrea Pitt
'RTA Allegations of Fraud in a Post-Jackson Era: The Handbook – 2nd Edition' by Andrew Mckie
'RTA Personal Injury Claims: A Practical Guide Post-Jackson' by Andrew Mckie
'On Experts: CPR35 for Lawyers and Experts' by David Boyle
'An Introduction to Personal Injury Law' by David Boyle

| 'A Practical Guide to Chronic Pain Claims' by Pankaj Madan |
| 'A Practical Guide to Claims Arising from Fatal Accidents' by James Patience |
| 'A Practical Guide to Subtle Brain Injury Claims' by Pankaj Madan |

These books and more are available to order online direct from the publisher at www.lawbriefpublishing.com, where you can also read free sample chapters. For any queries, contact us on 0844 587 2383 or mail@lawbriefpublishing.com.

Our books are also usually in stock at www.amazon.co.uk with free next day delivery for Prime members, and at good legal bookshops such as Wildy & Sons.

We are regularly launching new books in our series of practical day-to-day practitioners' guides. Visit our website and join our free newsletter to be kept informed and to receive special offers, free chapters, etc.

You can also follow us on Twitter at www.twitter.com/lawbriefpub.

Printed in Great Britain
by Amazon